Orlando   Boston   Dallas   Chicago   San Diego

Visit *The Learning Site!*
www.harcourtschool.com

ISBN 0-15-323517-9

19 20 21 22 054 10 09 08 07

Contents

ON YOUR MARK

Name **Emily Alvarenga**

▶ **Write the Vocabulary Word that best completes each sentence.**

colonel	soldiers	brambles	weary
outstretched	stumbling	urgent	

1. *Leaves* are to *vines* as *thorns* are to _brambles_.

2. *Closed* is to *open* as *shut tight* is to _outstretched_.

3. *Drink* is to *thirsty* as *rest* is to _weary_.

4. *Principal* is to *students* as _colonel_ is to *soldiers*.

5. *Small* is to *enormous* as *unimportant* is to _urgent_.

6. *Team* is to *players* as *army* is to _soldiers_.

7. *Speaking* is to *stuttering* as *running* is to _stumbling_.

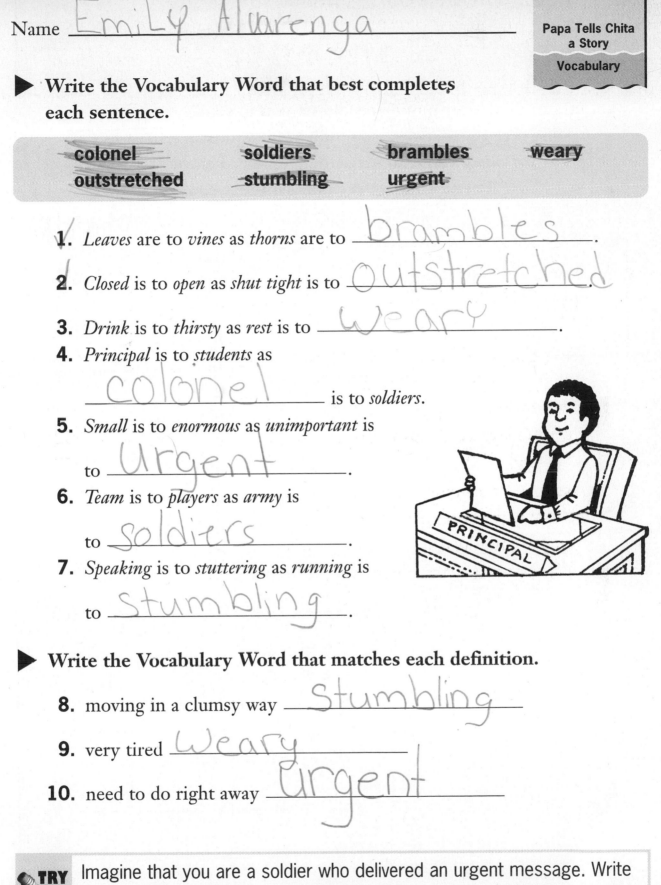

▶ **Write the Vocabulary Word that matches each definition.**

8. moving in a clumsy way _stumbling_

9. very tired _weary_

10. need to do right away _urgent_

TRY THIS! Imagine that you are a soldier who delivered an urgent message. Write a diary entry using Vocabulary Words. Tell what the message was about and what dangers you faced to deliver it.

Name _____

▶ **It's 1898. You are a reporter in Cuba writing a story
about a soldier. Your newspaper wants you to send
a one-line report every day, so you have to summarize
your journal entries into single sentences. Read each
journal entry. Then complete the one-sentence summary.**

1. July 14, 1898

Santiago, Cuba

A soldier volunteered to carry an important
message. He was to deliver it to troops on
the other side of the island. His name is
Private Grady.

A soldier volunteered
to carry an
an important message

2. July 15, 1898

Santiago, Cuba

Grady's trip was filled with danger, but
he made it safely across the island. He
won a medal for his bravery.

Grady trip was
filled with danger
but he made it
safly across the
Island and won
metal for his
bravery

2

© Harcourt

Name _____

▶ **Read the passage. Then circle the letter of the best answer to each question.**

July 15, 1898
Santiago, Cuba

Yesterday, Private Grady volunteered to travel across Cuba. He had to deliver an important message. The message was for Colonel Smith.

Grady's trip was very long and dangerous. He faced snakes and alligators along the way. After his horse ran away, he continued on foot. He walked on through mud and brambles.

Grady finally reached Colonel Smith. Grady gave him the message. Tomorrow, Private Grady will receive a medal for his bravery.

1 What is the main idea of the passage?

A Grady traveled across Cuba.

B Grady was ordered to deliver a message.

C Grady traveled across Cuba with an important message.

D Grady visited Colonel Smith.

> **Tip**
> The main idea can usually be found in the first or last sentence of a passage.

2 Which of the following is a fact that supports the author's idea that Grady's trip was "dangerous"?

F Grady escaped capture.

G Grady faced snakes and alligators.

H The trip was long.

J He stumbled through mud.

> **Tip**
> Choose the answer that gives details about a dangerous situation.

3 Which of the following summarizes the conclusion of the passage?

A Grady spoke to Colonel Smith.

B Grady delivered the message and will receive a medal.

C Grady traveled across Cuba with an important message.

D Grady will be given a medal.

> **Tip**
> Eliminate the answer that does not appear in the last paragraph.

SCHOOL-HOME CONNECTION Ask your child to tell you a story from a book or a movie, or about something that happened to him or her.

3

Practice Book
On Your Mark

© Harcourt

Name _____

▶ **Underline the figurative language in each sentence. Then rewrite the sentence without the figurative language.**

1. It was raining cats and dogs.

It's rainy hard.

2. There was a sea of mud on the street.

mud on thed streete. street

3. Papa ran like the wind.

ran like the wind.

4. He was covered in mud from head to toe.

mud from head to toe.

5. He wanted to sleep for a thousand years.

sleep for a thousand years

6. The alligator was as big as a house.

big as a house.

7. Papa swam through water that was as cold as ice.

was as cold as ice.

8. He was as strong as an ox.

strong as an ox.

© Harcourt

SCHOOL-HOME CONNECTION Read a favorite story aloud with your child. Help your child point out examples of figurative language, and discuss what they mean.

Practice Book
On Your Mark

Skill Reminder • An **adjective** is a word that describes a noun. An adjective can come before the noun it describes.
• An adjective can follow a verb such as *is* or *seems*.

▶ **Circle the adjective in each sentence. Underline the noun it describes.**

1. The frog jumped through the tall grass to the swamp.

2. There was a giant snake in the swamp.

3. The snake offered to give the frog a ride across the deep water.

4. "First promise not to eat me," said the worried frog.

5. "I promise," said the snake, with a big smile.

▶ **Think of an adjective to describe each underlined noun. Rewrite the sentence, adding the adjective.**

6. Papa was a <u>man</u>.

   _____

7. There was a <u>snake</u> in the grass.

   _____

8. A flag flew over the <u>house</u>.

   _____

9. She had to carry a <u>bag</u>.

   _____

10. Chita opened a <u>drawer</u> in the desk.

   _____

 List three items in your classroom. Use adjectives to describe them.

Skill Reminder The vowel sound you hear in *for* or *four* can be spelled *or, our,* or *ar.*

▶ Fold the paper along the dotted line. As each spelling word is read aloud, write it in the blank. Then unfold your paper, and check your work. Practice any spelling words you missed.

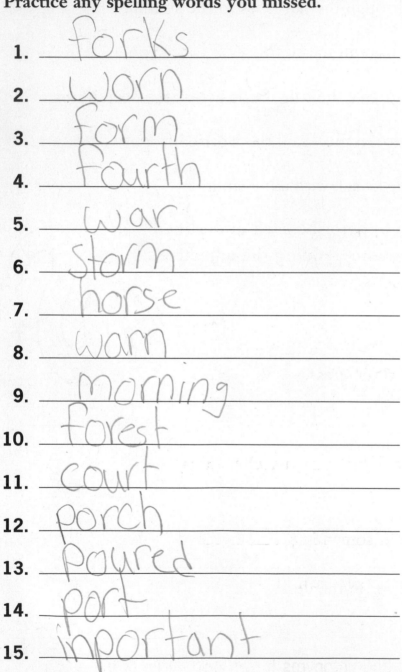

1. forks
2. worn
3. form
4. fourth
5. war
6. storm
7. horse
8. warn
9. morning
10. forest
11. court
12. porch
13. poured
14. port
15. important

SPELLING WORDS

1. forks
2. worn
3. form
4. fourth
5. war
6. storm
7. horse
8. warn
9. morning
10. forest
11. court
12. porch
13. poured
14. port
15. important

© Harcourt

Practice Book
On Your Mark

Name _____

▶ **Write the Vocabulary Word that best completes
each analogy.**

canyon   skillful   arranged   swiftly

gazing   pride   feast

1. *High* is to *low* as *mountain* is to ___canyon___.

2. *Laughter* is to *joke* as ___pride___ is to *winning*.

3. *Glad* is to *happy* as *quickly* is to ___swiftly___.

4. *Page* is to *book* as *food* is to ___feast___.

5. *Repaired* is to *fixed* as *sorted* is to ___arranged___.

6. *Feet* are to *walking* as *eyes* are to ___gazing___.

7. *Pupil* is to *student* as *expert* is to ___skillfull___.

▶ **Write the Vocabulary Word that matches each
definition below.**

8. taking a long look at something ___gazing___

9. able to do something very well ___pride___

10. celebration with lots of food ___feast___

TRY THIS! Think of synonyms and antonyms for at least three of the
Vocabulary Words.

7

© Harcourt

Name Emily

▶ **Read the passage below. Then circle the letter of the best answer to each question.**

Some stars are hot and big. They are called red giants. Others are small and cool. They are called white dwarfs. Most stars do not have any planets. Did you know that our sun is a star? It has planets, such as Earth and Mars, revolving around it. Many astronomers say that the sun is a typical star. It is made up of the same material as other stars. It moves and gives off heat in the same way other stars of its size do. Over billions of years, the sun will change just the way other stars change. People describe the ways a star changes as the life of a star. Stars grow very slowly. Eventually, stars become so big and hot that they use up all the special gases they need to glow. Without the special gases, the red giants get smaller and cooler, and eventually turn into white dwarfs.

1 How are the sun, a red giant, and a white dwarf alike?
  A They are all stars.
  B They are close to Earth.
  C They are the same size.
  D They are small and cool.

> **Tip**
> Find the main idea of the passage to help you answer this question.

2 What is the difference between a red giant and a white dwarf?
  F A red giant gives off heat, but a white dwarf traps heat.
  G A red giant is big and hot, and a white dwarf is small and cool.
  H A red giant changes over millions of years, but a white dwarf doesn't.
  J A red giant is a star, and a white dwarf is a planet.

> **Tip**
> Remember, *difference* means what is **not** alike.

3 How is the sun *unlike* a typical star?
  A It changes over time.
  B It uses gases to give off heat.
  C It has planets.
  D It grows slowly.

> **Tip**
> What makes the sun different from most stars?

8

© Harcourt

Name _____

HOMEWORK
Coyote Places
the Stars

Compare and
Contrast
TEST PREP

▶ **Read the advertisements. Then write the things that are alike and the things that are different in the chart.**

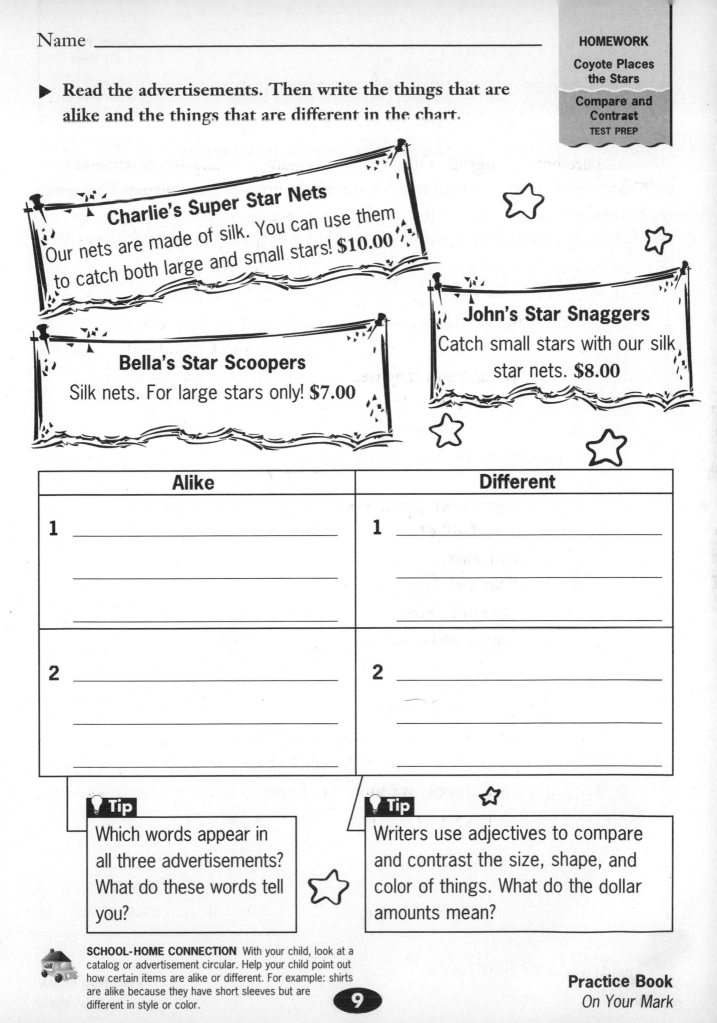

Charlie's Super Star Nets
Our nets are made of silk. You can use them to catch both large and small stars! **$10.00**

Bella's Star Scoopers
Silk nets. For large stars only! **$7.00**

John's Star Snaggers
Catch small stars with our silk star nets. **$8.00**

Alike	Different
1 _____	1 _____
2 _____	2 _____

💡 **Tip**
Which words appear in all three advertisements? What do these words tell you?

💡 **Tip**
Writers use adjectives to compare and contrast the size, shape, and color of things. What do the dollar amounts mean?

SCHOOL-HOME CONNECTION With your child, look at a catalog or advertisement circular. Help your child point out how certain items are alike or different. For example: shirts are alike because they have short sleeves but are different in style or color.

9

Practice Book
On Your Mark

© Harcourt

Name _____

Skill Reminder Some **adjectives** tell what kind. Adjectives can describe size, shape, or color. Adjectives can describe how something looks, sounds, feels, tastes, or smells.

▶ **Circle the adjective in each sentence. Underline the noun it describes.**

1. Zog was a horrible monster.

2. He flew his fast spaceship.

3. He was a very good pilot.

4. He never crashed into any big stars.

5. Zog liked to fly through the bright sky.

▶ **Think of an adjective to describe each underlined noun. Rewrite each sentence, adding the adjective**

6. Max looked up at the moon.

_____

7. He thought it was made of cheese.

_____

8. He bought a telescope to take a better look.

_____

9. He saw a cow on the moon.

_____

10. The cow was doing a dance.

_____

Practice Book
On Your Mark

Name _____

Skill Reminder **Homophones** are words that sound the same but have different spellings and meanings.

▶ Fold the paper along the dotted line. As each spelling word is read aloud, write it in the blank. Then unfold your paper, and check your work. Practice spelling any words you missed.

1. hear
2. here
3. flour
4. flower
5. won
6. One
7. way
8. wiegh
9. herd
10. heard
11. Our
12. beat
13. beet
14. hair
15. hare

SPELLING WORDS

1. won
2. one
3. weigh
4. way
5. heard
6. herd
7. our
8. flour
9. flower
10. here
11. hear
12. beat
13. beet
14. hair
15. hare

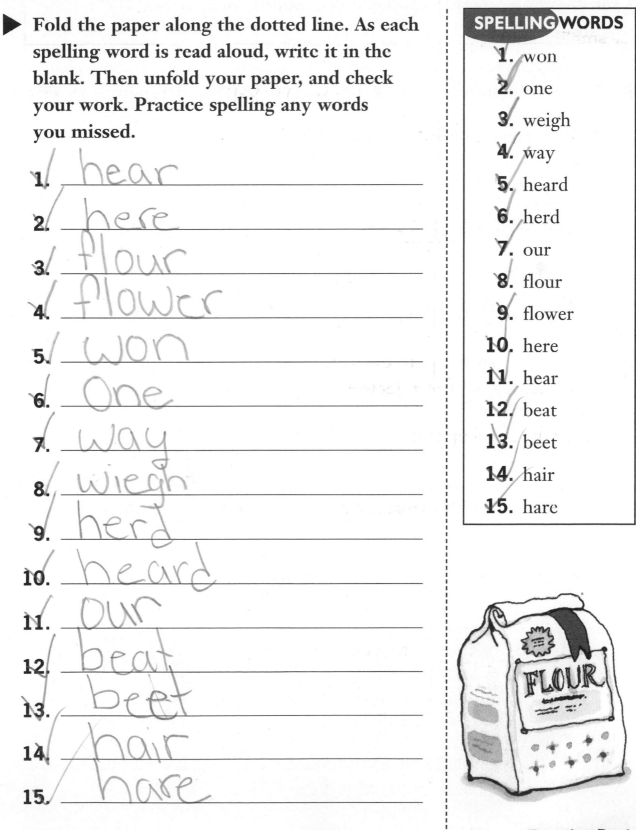

Practice Book
On Your Mark

▶ **Complete each animal's sentence with the best Vocabulary Word.**

| nonsense | tidbit | mischief | duty | council | satisfied |

1. **Rabbit:** I wonder what the _____council_____ meeting is all about.

2. **Frog:** I don't know. I haven't even heard a _____tidbit_____ of information about it.

3. **Iguana:** Maybe I've been making too much _____nonsense_____ by teasing the mosquito.

4. **Turtle:** No, Iguana. We are meeting because it is my _____duty_____ to tell you that you have been making a buzzing sound in your sleep.

5. **Iguana:** I don't buzz in my sleep! That's complete _____mischief_____.

6. **Owl:** I am not _____satisfied_____ with your answer, Iguana. I'm sure I heard a *ze-ze-ze* sound coming from your place last night.

TRY THIS! Write an ending to the story in numbers 1 through 6 above. Use as many Vocabulary Words as you can.

Name _____

HOMEWORK

Why Mosquitoes
Buzz in
People's Ears

Summarize
TEST PREP

▶ **Read the paragraph. Then circle the letter of the best answer to each question.**

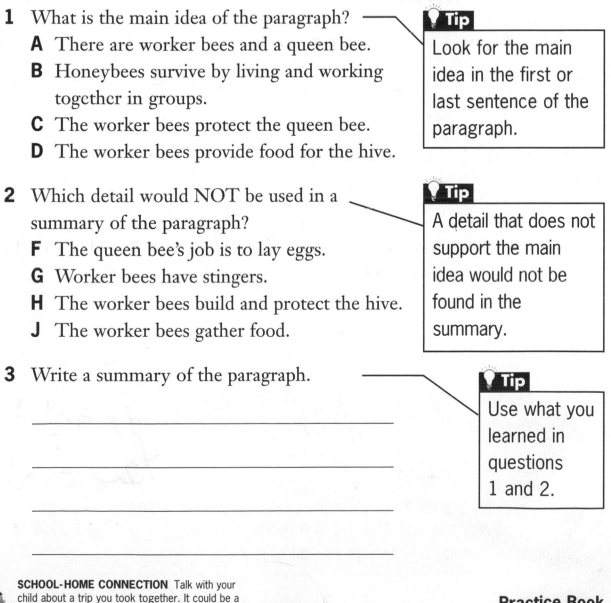

HONEYBEES

Like humans, honeybees live and work in groups. These groups are called colonies. A colony has one queen bee and many worker bees. One job of the worker bees is to build a hive. They also gather honey to feed the other bees. In addition, they protect the colony with their stingers. The queen bee's job is to lay eggs so that there are enough bees to take care of the colony. Honeybees need each other to survive. All the bees in the community work together to make their hive a home.

1 What is the main idea of the paragraph?
  A There are worker bees and a queen bee.
  B Honeybees survive by living and working together in groups.
  C The worker bees protect the queen bee.
  D The worker bees provide food for the hive.

💡 **Tip**
Look for the main idea in the first or last sentence of the paragraph.

2 Which detail would NOT be used in a summary of the paragraph?
  F The queen bee's job is to lay eggs.
  G Worker bees have stingers.
  H The worker bees build and protect the hive.
  J The worker bees gather food.

💡 **Tip**
A detail that does not support the main idea would not be found in the summary.

3 Write a summary of the paragraph.

_____

_____

_____

_____

💡 **Tip**
Use what you learned in questions 1 and 2.

SCHOOL-HOME CONNECTION Talk with your child about a trip you took together. It could be a trip to the store or a trip to visit a relative. Then ask your child to write a summary of the story

13

Practice Book
On Your Mark

© Harcourt

Name _____

Why Mosquitoes
Buzz in People's
Ears

Grammar:
Adjectives for
How Many

Skill Reminder   Some **adjectives** tell *how many*. Not all adjectives that tell how many give an exact number.

▶ **Circle the adjective in each sentence. Underline the noun it describes.**

    1. The mosquito bothered many animals.

    2. Ken's rabbit had several carrots for dinner.

    3. Two snakes escaped from the zoo.

    4. The monkey stole all the bananas.

    5. Each animal sang a song in the zoo talent show.

▶ **Think of an adjective to describe each underlined noun. The adjective should tell how many. Rewrite each sentence, adding the adjective.**

    6. I saw <u>animals</u> at the zoo.

    _____

    7. The <u>monkeys</u> were having a banana party.

    _____

    8. They were dancing on <u>banana peels</u>.

    _____

    9. <u>Iguanas</u> complained about the noise.

    _____

    10. <u>Monkeys</u> like to swing through the trees.

    _____

TRY THIS!   Describe the kinds of groceries you have in your kitchen, using adjectives that tell how many. For example, you may have *many* boxes of cereal, *two* cans of soup, or *several* green peppers.

© Harcourt

Practice Book
On Your Mark

Name _____

Skill Reminder The vowel sound you hear in *her*, *stir*, and *fur* can be spelled *er*, *ir*, or *ur*.

▶ Fold the paper along the dotted line. As each spelling word is read aloud, write it in the blank. Then unfold your paper, and check your work. Practice spelling any words you missed.

1. curl
2. birth
3. burnd
4. perfect
5. church
6. thirty
7. firm
8. skirt
9. clerk
10. jerked
11. dirt
12. shirt
13. person
14. purse
15. term

SPELLING WORDS

1. curl
2. birth
3. burned
4. perfect
5. thirty
6. church
7. firm
8. skirt
9. clerk
10. jerked
11. dirt
12. shirt
13. person
14. purse
15. term

Practice Book
On Your Mark

▶ **Write the Vocabulary Word that best completes each sentence.**

| ~~latch~~ | ~~dusk~~ | cunning | ~~embraced~~ | ~~tender~~ | brittle | ~~delighted~~ |

1. An old man worked from dawn until ___dusk___ in the fields.

2. He opened the ___brittle___ of the gate in front of his house.

3. His ___cunning___, old, blind dog knew it was him by the sound of his footsteps.

4. The old man gave the dog a ___tender___ bone.

5. His wife was cooking a ___latch___ piece of meat for dinner.

6. The man ___embrace___ his wife.

7. They were all ___delighted___ by the good meal at the end of the day.

TRY THIS! Use the Vocabulary Words to make up a story. Have one character try to trick another character to get something, such as an item of clothing or a treat to eat.

Practice Book
On Your Mark

Name _____

▶ **Read the two story endings. Then fill in the chart below. List details that are the same and details that are different.**

Story Ending #1

"Grandmother, what big ears you have!" Little Red Riding Hood said as she entered her grandmother's cottage. "All the better to hear you with, my dear," replied the wolf, who was dressed in Grandmother's clothing. Little Red Riding Hood exclaimed, "But Grandmother, what big teeth you have!" Then the wolf said, "All the better to eat you with, my dear!" The wolf jumped up and chased Little Red Riding Hood out the door.

Story Ending #2

"I have some treats for you," Little Pink Riding Hood said as she entered her grandmother's castle. "Good!" said the wolf, who was dressed in grandmother's clothing. "I am very hungry." Little Pink Riding Hood realized at once that this was not her grandmother. She became very scared. "I brought you some chocolate chip cookies, but I left them outside in my backpack," Little Pink Riding Hood said. "I'll go get them." She backed away and ran out of her grandmother's house.

	Alike	Different
Character	1 little red riding hood	4 • wolf •
Plot	2	5 • •
Setting	3	6 • •

SCHOOL-HOME CONNECTION With your child, talk about the book and the movie or television versions of a favorite story. Discuss the ways they are the same and different.

17

Practice Book
On Your Mark

© Harcourt

Name _____

Skill Reminder   The words *a, an,* and *the* are called
articles. Use *a* and *an* for singular nouns. Use *the* for both singular
and plural nouns. Use *a* before a word that begins with a consonant
sound. Use *an* before a word that begins with a vowel sound.

▶ **Circle the article in each sentence.
Underline the noun it introduces.**

   1. Remember to lock the door
      after I leave.

   2. Keep a candle lit until I come home.

   3. If you hear someone ringing the
      doorbell, don't answer.

   4. It could be an animal trying to trick you.

   5. There may be a wolf outside who wants to get in.

▶ **Complete each sentence, filling in each blank with *a, an,* or *the.***

   6. _____ Big Bad Wolf wanted to learn how to
      drive a car.

   7. He was tired of riding _____ bicycle.

   8. He went to _____ only driving school in his town.

   9. He brought his teacher _____ apple.

   10. His teacher gave him _____ good grade.

 **TRY
THIS!**   Decide whether to use *a* or *an* in front of each of these five words:
grandmother, evening, wolf, animal, and *trick.* Then use each phrase
aloud in a sentence.

Practice Book
On Your Mark

Skill Reminder Some two-syllable words have double consonants in the middle. Words like this are often divided into two syllables between the two like consonants: but•ter.

▶ Fold the paper along the dotted line. As each spelling word is read aloud, write it in the blank. Then unfold your paper, and check your work. Practice spelling any words you missed.

SPELLING WORDS

1. pulled
2. begged
3. hugged
4. silly
5. correct
6. latter
7. matter
8. supper
9. common
10. lesson
11. collect
12. setting
13. bottles
14. different
15. jelly

1. _____

2. _____

3. _____

4. _____

5. _____

6. _____

7. _____

8. _____

9. _____

10. _____

11. _____

12. _____

13. _____

14. _____

15. _____

© Harcourt

Practice Book
On Your Mark

▶ **Rewrite each sentence. Replace the underlined word(s) with the best Vocabulary Word.**

~~wits~~   ~~wailing~~   ~~advice~~   dreadful   faring   ~~farewell~~

Dear Sonya,

1. I will not listen to your <u>smart ideas</u> ever again.

I will not listen to your advice ever again.

2. You said that I should be nicer to my <u>horrible</u> little brother.

You said that I should be nicer to my dreadful little brother

3. You forgot to tell what to do to get him to stop <u>crying</u>.

You forgot to tell what to do to get to spot wailing.

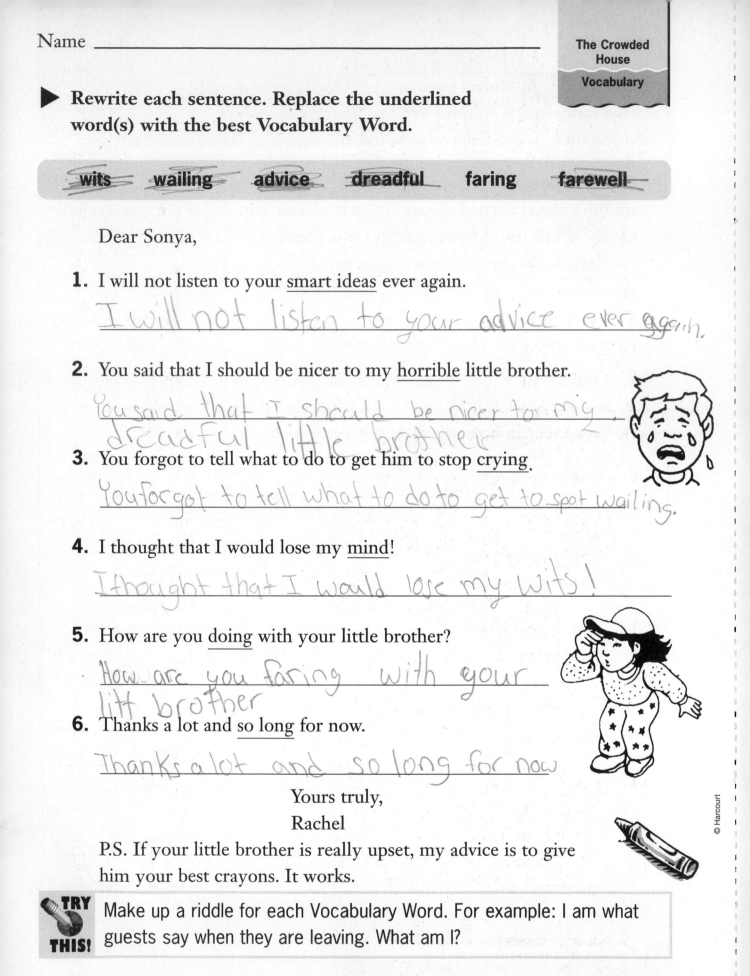

4. I thought that I would lose my <u>mind</u>!

I thought that I would lose my wits!

5. How are you <u>doing</u> with your little brother?

How are you faring with your litt brother

6. Thanks a lot and <u>so long</u> for now.

Thanks a lot and so long for now

Yours truly,
Rachel

P.S. If your little brother is really upset, my advice is to give him your best crayons. It works.

TRY THIS! Make up a riddle for each Vocabulary Word. For example: I am what guests say when they are leaving. What am I?

Practice Book
On Your Mark

▶ **Read each paragraph. Then circle the letter of the best answer to each question.**

X   Billy Goat and Harry Goat lived in a very crowded house. Billy Goat filled his half of the house with For Real Kids Only games and 379 toy stuffed animals. Harry Goat collected sticks and rocks of every shape and size. The last time Harry Goat counted, he had 973 rocks in his collection.

Y   Good manners are very important in a crowded movie theater. The people around you can hear you even when you whisper. In fact, they can hear you every time you tear open a candy wrapper. The person in front of you will get angry if you swing your legs and kick the back of the seat.

Z   Too much weight in an elevator can cause it to break. A sign inside every public elevator tells how many people can ride safely at one time. An elevator that can hold 13 adults can carry a weight of 2,000 pounds.

1   What is the author's purpose in paragraph X?
  A to entertain
  B to inform by giving facts
  C to inform by telling how to do something
  D to persuade

> 💡 **Tip**
> Sometimes an author tells made-up facts for fun.

2   What is the author's purpose in paragraph Y?
  F to entertain
  G to inform by giving facts
  H to inform by telling how to do something
  J to persuade

> 💡 **Tip**
> Compare this paragraph to the others. How is it different?

3   What is the author's purpose in paragraph Z?
  A to entertain
  B to inform by giving facts
  C to inform by telling how to do something
  D to persuade

> 💡 **Tip**
> Ignore the choices you know are wrong.

SCHOOL-HOME CONNECTION With your child, look at a newspaper. Discuss the clues, such as the title, pictures, and first paragraph, that tell the author's purpose. Ask your child to clip three articles, each with a different purpose, and label the clippings with the author's purpose.

Practice Book
On Your Mark

© Harcourt

Name _____

Skill Reminder • Adjectives can describe by comparing people, animals, places, or things.
• Use *-er, more,* or *less* with adjectives to compare two things.
• Use *-est, most,* or *least* with adjectives to compare more than two things.

▶ Read the choices of adjectives in parentheses ( ) in each sentence. Then underline the correct one.

1. Our house is even **(more crowded, the most crowded)** than your house.

2. In fact, our house is **(more crowded, the most crowded)** one in town.

3. Our donkey is **(tallest, taller)** than our goat.

4. The chickens are **(the loudest, louder)** of all our animals.

5. I was **(less pleased, the least pleased)** when the animals came than I was when they left.

▶ Rewrite each sentence, using the correct form of the adjective in parentheses ( ).

6. The **(young)** of the eight children was in bed.

_____

7. Our goat is **(small)** than our donkey.

_____

8. Mother is **(unhappy)** than Father about the crowding.

_____

9. Cameron is **(fast)** than we are.

_____

10. Blythe had the **(wonderful)** idea of all.

_____

Practice Book
On Your Mark

Name _____

Skill Reminder • Words that end with two consonants do not change before you add an -er or -est ending.

• If a word ends in e, drop the e and add -er or -est.

• If a word has a short vowel and ends in a single consonant, double the consonant. Then add -er or -est.

▶ Fold the paper along the dotted line. As each spelling word is read aloud, write it in the blank. Then unfold your paper, and check your work. Practice spelling any words you missed.

1. faster
2. wisest
3. bigger
4. slowest
5. cooler
6. hottest
7. soonest
8. shorter
9. kindest
10. louder
11. slimmer
12. wildest
13. tamer
14. whitest
15. strangest

SPELLING WORDS

1. faster
2. wisest
3. bigger
4. slowest
5. cooler
6. hottest
7. soonest
8. shorter
9. kindest
10. louder
11. slimmer
12. wildest
13. tamer
14. whitest
15. strangest

Practice Book
On Your Mark

Name _____

▶ **Read each sentence. Choose the Vocabulary Word that has the same meaning as the underlined word(s). Then, write each sentence using the Vocabulary Word.**

| glistened | county | galloped | clutched | bid | auctioneer |

1. Juno was the most beautiful pony in our <u>part of the state</u>.

_____

2. Her brown and white coat <u>glowed</u> in the sun.

_____

3. I loved to watch Juno as she <u>ran fast</u> through the fields.

_____

4. The <u>leader of the auction</u> knew the farmers wanted big horses.

_____

5. I was happy when I made the only <u>offer to buy</u>.

_____

6. When they put Juno's reins in my hand, <u>I grasped</u> them.

_____

▶ **Write the Vocabulary Word that best completes each sentence.**

The pony **(7)** _____ across the

meadow. Lauren **(8)** _____

the reins. She had bought Juno at the **(9)** _____ fair.

She made the highest **(10)** _____ for the pony.

24

▶ **Read the page from an auction catalog. Then read statements 1–10. Circle *fact* or *opinion*. If you circle *opinion*, write the reason for your choice.**

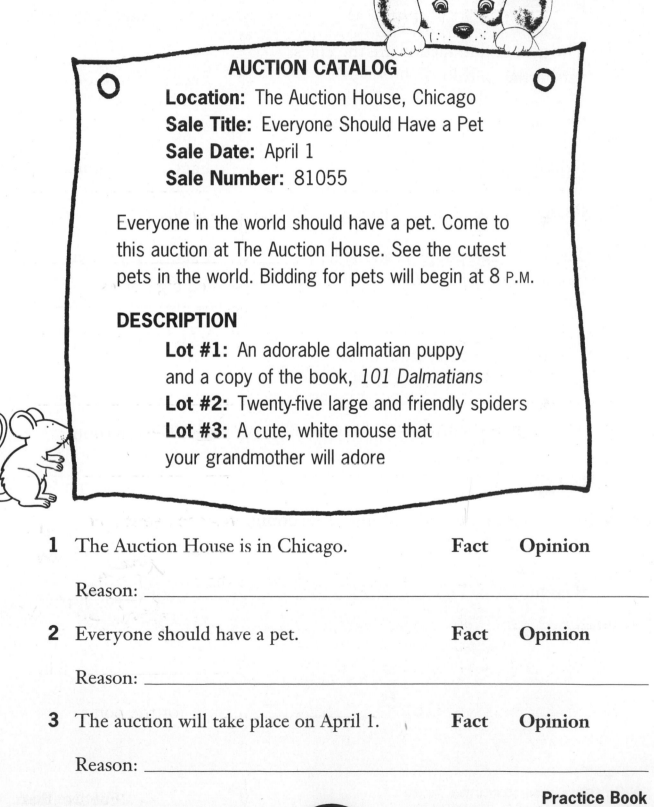

AUCTION CATALOG

Location: The Auction House, Chicago
Sale Title: Everyone Should Have a Pet
Sale Date: April 1
Sale Number: 81055

Everyone in the world should have a pet. Come to this auction at The Auction House. See the cutest pets in the world. Bidding for pets will begin at 8 P.M.

DESCRIPTION

Lot #1: An adorable dalmatian puppy and a copy of the book, *101 Dalmatians*
Lot #2: Twenty-five large and friendly spiders
Lot #3: A cute, white mouse that your grandmother will adore

1 The Auction House is in Chicago.   **Fact   Opinion**

Reason: _____

2 Everyone should have a pet.   **Fact   Opinion**

Reason: _____

3 The auction will take place on April 1.   **Fact   Opinion**

Reason: _____

4 The title of the sale is "Everyone Should
Have a Pet."   **Fact   Opinion**

Reason: _____

5 The pets at this auction are the cutest
pets in the world.   **Fact   Opinion**

Reason: _____

6 Bidding will begin at 8 P.M.   **Fact   Opinion**

Reason: _____

7 The dalmatian puppy is adorable.   **Fact   Opinion**

Reason: _____

8 The spiders are large.   **Fact   Opinion**

Reason: _____

9 The spiders are friendly.   **Fact   Opinion**

Reason: _____

10 All grandmothers will love the white
mouse for sale.   **Fact   Opinion**

Reason: _____

SCHOOL-HOME CONNECTION With your
child, write three facts and make up three
opinion statements about an animal.

26

Practice Book
On Your Mark

© Harcourt

Skill Reminder • The **verb** is the main word in the predicate of a sentence.

• An **action verb** tells what the subject of the sentence does.

▶ Circle the action verb in each sentence.

1. Leah rode her pony to the store.

2. The little pony kicked a stone.

3. The storekeeper admired the pony.

4. He bought the pony from Leah.

5. Later, he returned the pony to her.

▶ Write a verb from the box to complete each sentence.

stopped	sweeps	offered	stared	galloped

6. Leah _____ away on her pony.

7. She _____ in front of Mr. B.'s store.

8. Mr. B. _____ his front steps every day.

9. Leah _____ to sell her pony to Mr. B.

10. Mr. B. _____ at Leah in surprise.

 TRY THIS! Find three interesting verbs that you could use in place of the verb *walked*. Write three sentences using your new verbs.

Practice Book
On Your Mark

Name _____

Skill Reminder   A compound word is formed by joining
two smaller words.

▶ Fold the paper along the dotted line. As each
spelling word is read aloud, write it in the
blank. Then unfold your paper, and check
your work. Practice spelling any words
you missed.

1. _____

2. _____

3. _____

4. _____

5. _____

6. _____

7. _____

8. _____

9. _____

10. _____

11. _____

12. _____

13. _____

14. _____

15. _____

SPELLING WORDS

1. sometimes
2. pickup
3. dishwater
4. notebook
5. upstairs
6. football
7. sunshine
8. outdoors
9. hallway
10. timeout
11. doorway
12. sunset
13. bookcase
14. everyone
15. everything

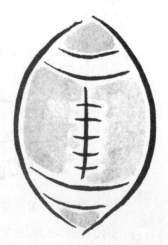

© Harcourt

28

Name _____

▶ **Write the Vocabulary Word that matches each definition.**

| ranchers | profit | tending | corral | stray | market |

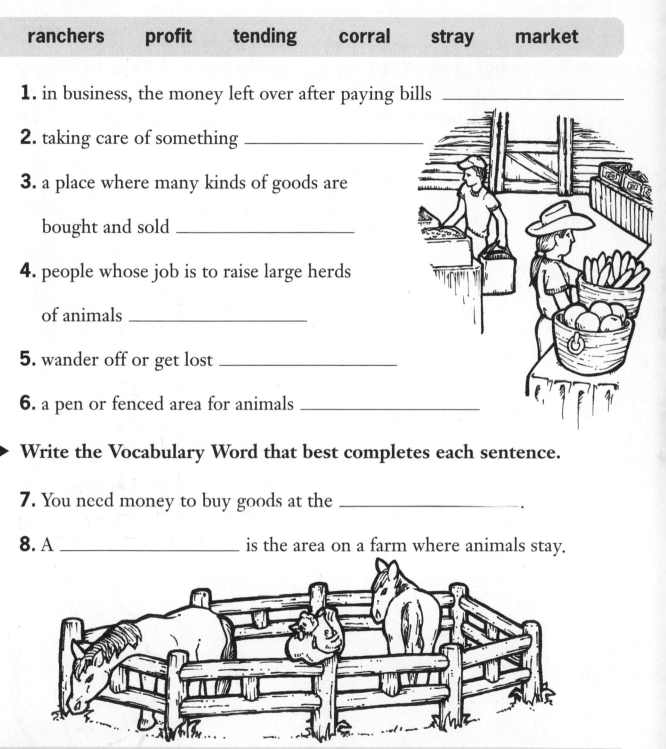

1. in business, the money left over after paying bills _____

2. taking care of something _____

3. a place where many kinds of goods are

bought and sold _____

4. people whose job is to raise large herds

of animals _____

5. wander off or get lost _____

6. a pen or fenced area for animals _____

▶ **Write the Vocabulary Word that best completes each sentence.**

7. You need money to buy goods at the _____ .

8. A _____ is the area on a farm where animals stay.

 TRY THIS! Write a story about a ranch that raises cattle. See if you can use all of the Vocabulary Words.

Practice Book
On Your Mark

Name _____

▶ **Read the traditional cowboy song below. Then circle the letter of the best answer to each question.**

Home on the Range (1867)

1st Verse

Oh, give me a home where the buffalo roam,
Where the deer and the antelope play,
Where seldom is heard a discouraging word,
And the skies are not cloudy all day.

Chorus

Home, home on the range,
Where the deer and the antelope play,
Where seldom is heard a discouraging word,
And the skies are not cloudy all day.

2nd Verse

Where the air is so pure, and the zephyrs are free,
And the breezes so balmy and light,
That I would not exchange my home on the range,
For all of the cities so bright.

3rd Verse

How often at night, when the heavens are bright,
With the light from the glittering stars,
Have I stood there amazed, and asked as I gazed,
If their glory exceeds that of ours.

Name _____

1 What is the main idea of the song?

A A cowboy needs a new home.

B Cowboys are homeless.

C Cowboys think of the range as home.

D Cowboys don't like cloudy weather.

> **Tip**
> The title may reflect the main idea.

2 One reason cowboys like their home is

F it is very quiet.

G the sky is clear.

H the weather is terrible.

J deer and antelope stay out of sight.

> **Tip**
> Eliminate answers that are clearly wrong.

3 Another reason cowboys like their home is

A the people are not discouraging.

B it is very clean.

C the mountains are beautiful.

D the food is great.

> **Tip**
> Which choice is supported by the lyrics?

4 Why do cowboys love the range?

F The winds are very strong.

G There is no pollution.

H It is close to the city.

J The zephyrs are not free.

> **Tip**
> The answer may not be stated directly. It may be implied.

5 What do cowboys love about the range at night?

A the headlights from cars

B the restaurants

C television

D the stars

> **Tip**
> Consider the year when the lyrics were written.

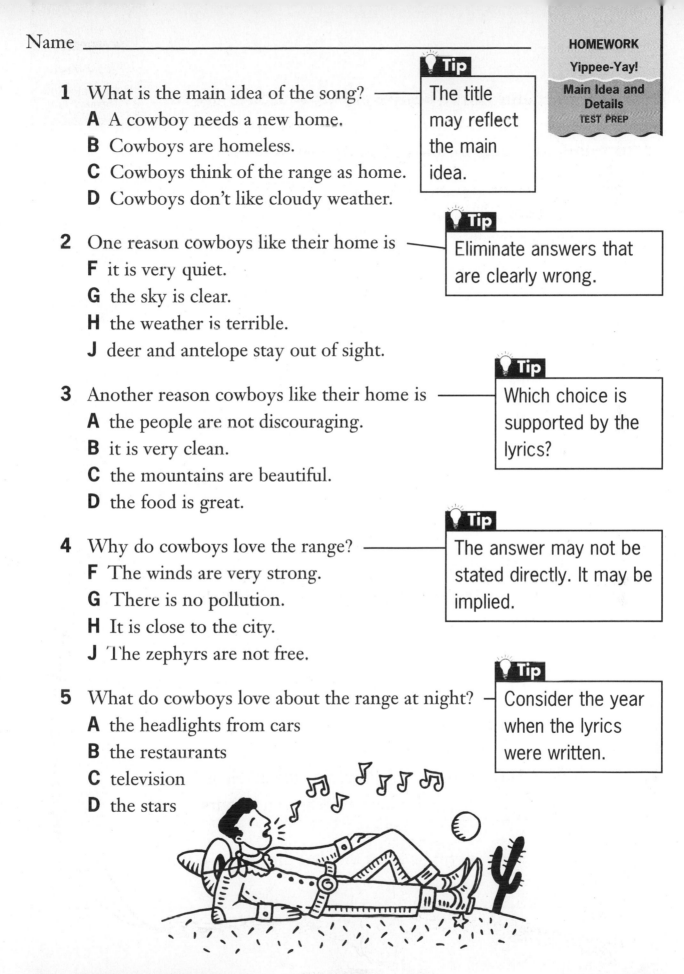

SCHOOL-HOME CONNECTION With your child, write a song about the place that you call home.

31

Practice Book
On Your Mark

© Harcourt

Name _____

▶ **Write the name of the best reference source to use to answer each question. Hint: You can find the answers to some questions in more than one source.**

1. Is Texas east or west of Arizona? _____

2. What is a longhorn steer and what does it look like?

_____

3. What kind of weather does Santa Fe, New Mexico have?

_____

4. How long have ranchers been raising cattle in the United States?

_____

5. What is the meaning of the word *corral*?

_____

6. What was the population of Dallas, Texas, last year?

_____

7. How is the word *lariat* pronounced? _____

8. What states border New Mexico? _____

9. How far is Dallas, Texas, from the South Pole?

_____

10. What is a synonym, or word that has the same meaning, as *stray?*

_____

SCHOOL-HOME CONNECTION With your child, make a list of three questions inspired by the story. Help your child make a plan to answer the questions by looking them up at school or at home.

Practice Book
On Your Mark

Name _____

Skill Reminder A helping verb works with the main
verb to tell about an action. The words *have, has,* and
had are often used as helping verbs.

▶ **Circle the helping verb in each sentence.**

1. A cowboy and a farmer were looking for gold.

2. The two friends had lost their way in the forest.

3. A map should help them.

4. The cowboy could read a compass.

5. They would not find gold, but they found their way home.

▶ **Complete each sentence with *have* or *has*.**

6. The children _____ seen the cattle thieves.

7. Their mother _____ shown them a picture of the robbers.

8. The sheriff _____ hung up "Wanted" posters.

9. Everyone in town _____ looked at the pictures.

10. The cowboys _____ caught the cattle stealers.

▶ **Complete each sentence with a helping verb and the correct form of
the main verb in parentheses ( ).**

11. The cowgirl and the cowboy _____ at the
    hoedown. **(dance)**

12. The rider _____ onto the back of a wild
    steer. **(climb)**

33

Skill Reminder **Some words have the VCCV spelling pattern, as in *napkin* and *enjoy*.**

▶ Fold the paper along the dotted line. As each spelling word is read aloud, write it in the blank. Then unfold your paper, and check your work. Practice spelling any words you missed.

1. _____

2. _____

3. _____

4. _____

5. _____

6. _____

7. _____

8. _____

9. _____

10. _____

11. _____

12. _____

13. _____

14. _____

15. _____

SPELLING WORDS

1. cowboy
2. horses
3. corral
4. winter
5. always
6. cactus
7. garden
8. tender
9. window
10. basket
11. fifteen
12. lasso
13. market
14. until
15. Monday

Name _____

▶ **Write the Vocabulary Word that best completes each sentence.**

| stagecoach | miners | nuggets | skillet |
| settle | boom town | landmark | |

1. The _____ took twenty-one days to reach California.

2. Amanda's family decided to _____ in a tiny town.

3. Nearby, _____ were digging deep into the earth for gold.

4. Some miners found raw lumps of gold called _____.

5. Amanda baked her pie in a _____.

6. The _____ they were building in the town could be seen from far away.

7. The town grew so fast it could be called a _____.

TRY THIS! Draw a picture of a mining town, illustrating at least three of the Vocabulary Words.

© Harcourt

Practice Book
On Your Mark

Name _____

▶ **Read diary entries. Think about which statements are facts and which are opinions. In the chart below, write three facts from Jose's diary and three facts from Jessie's diary. Then write three opinions from each diary.**

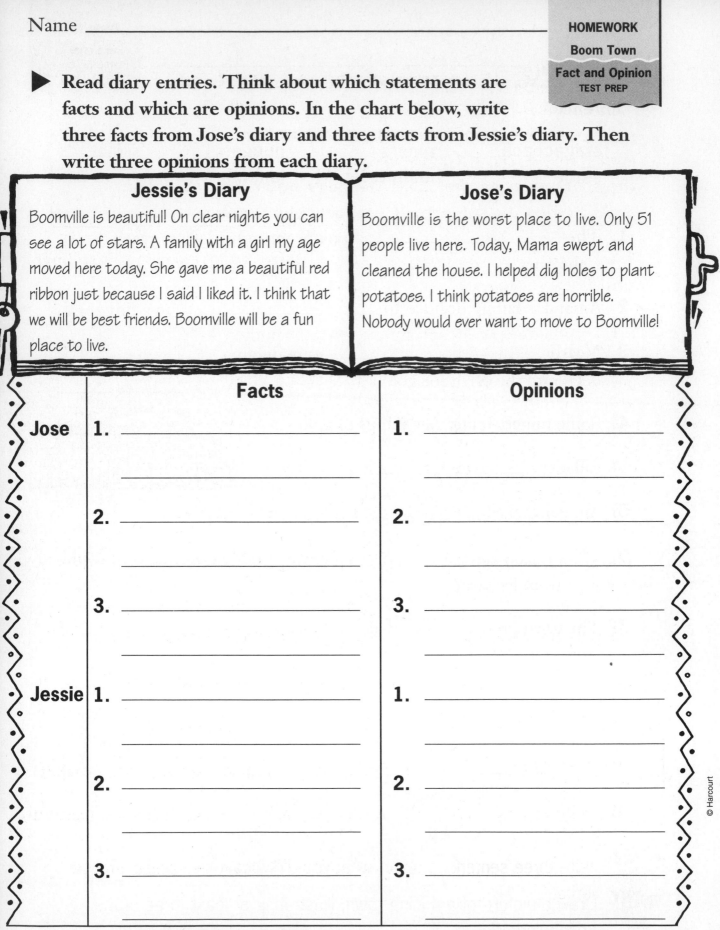

Jessie's Diary

Boomville is beautiful! On clear nights you can see a lot of stars. A family with a girl my age moved here today. She gave me a beautiful red ribbon just because I said I liked it. I think that we will be best friends. Boomville will be a fun place to live.

Jose's Diary

Boomville is the worst place to live. Only 51 people live here. Today, Mama swept and cleaned the house. I helped dig holes to plant potatoes. I think potatoes are horrible. Nobody would ever want to move to Boomville!

Facts

Opinions

Jose

1. _____

2. _____

3. _____

Jessie

1. _____

2. _____

3. _____

1. _____

2. _____

3. _____

1. _____

2. _____

3. _____

SCHOOL-HOME CONNECTION Invite your child to write a brief diary entry about his or her day. Write a brief description of your own day. Then, as you read and discuss your diary entries, ask your child to write an "F" over each fact and an "O" over each opinion statement.

36

Practice Book
On Your Mark

© Harcourt

Name _____

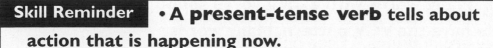
Skill Reminder • **A present-tense verb** tells about action that is happening now.
• A verb must *agree* with its subject in number.
• Add *-s* or *-es* to most present-tense verbs when the subject of the sentence is *he, she, it,* or a singular noun. Do not add an ending when the subject is *I, you,* or a plural noun.

▶ Underline the verb in each sentence. Write *S* above a singular subject and *P* above a plural subject.

1. Peddler Pete roams from one town to another.

2. Travelers shop at Peddler Pete's Trading Post.

3. They come to our cabin.

4. The town needs a laundry.

5. Sometimes the line of people snakes around the house.

▶ Complete each sentence with the correct present-tense form of the verb in parentheses ( ).

6. My father _____ in the gold fields. **(work)**

7. I _____ to make a pie in a skillet. **(decide)**

8. Gooseberries _____ on bushes. **(grow)**

9. Amanda _____ pies she can sell to the miners. **(bake)**

10. Peddler Pete _____ his beard when he thinks. **(scratch)**

Write three sentences about what you did today. Use present-tense verbs.

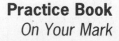
Practice Book
On Your Mark

Skill Reminder Many words with a long vowel sound in the first syllable have the **VCV** pattern. Many words that begin with *be-* have the **VCV** pattern.

▶ Fold the paper along the dotted line. As each spelling word is read aloud, write it in the blank. Then unfold your paper, and check your work. Practice spelling any words you missed.

1. _____

2. _____

3. _____

4. _____

5. _____

6. _____

7. _____

8. _____

9. _____

10. _____

11. _____

12. _____

13. _____

14. _____

15. _____

SPELLING WORDS

1. belong
2. hotel
3. focus
4. miner
5. pupil
6. begin
7. music
8. future
9. behind
10. tiger
11. become
12. motel
13. baker
14. cabin
15. ocean

© Harcourt

Practice Book
On Your Mark

Name _____

▶ **Read each group of words listed below. Then write
the Vocabulary Word that belongs in each group.**

trading	schooner	harvest	machete
pulp	bargain	support	

1. soft part
meat

_____

2. help
hold up

_____

3. buying and selling
exchanging

_____

4. knife
sword

_____

5. ship
sailboat

_____

6. pick
gather

_____

7. make a deal
agree to buy

_____

▶ **Answer each riddle with a Vocabulary Word.**

8. I am a sharp tool used for cutting.

What am I? a _____

9. I am a large boat that may be used for carrying goods

to other places. What am I? a _____

10. I am the soft, mushy part of a fruit or vegetable.

What am I? the _____

39

Name _____

▶ **Read the two fictional speeches. Then circle the letter of the best answer to each question.**

Speech 1

JOHN: I found him on Main Street. He looked so sad, and he was limping. I couldn't leave him there, Mom. I'll put up signs saying we've found a dog, but if no one calls, can we keep him? Please? He can sleep in my room, and I'll feed him every day.

Speech 2

ROSA: Mama! Look! I found a hermit crab. I know I have to return it to the ocean, but I wanted you to see that I caught this one without anyone's help.

1 Both John and Rosa
 A are afraid of animals.
 B like animals.
 C like to go to Main Street.
 D like to help lost animals.

> **Tip**
> The question is about what John and Rosa have in common.

2 Which statement is most likely true?
 F John lives in the country, and Rosa lives in the city.
 G Rosa and John both live in the city.
 H John and Rosa both live in the country.
 J John lives in a small town, and Rosa lives near a beach.

> **Tip**
> Find words that give geographic clues.

3 Which statement is true?
 A Both children wish to keep the animals they find as pets.
 B Rosa wants to keep the crab, but John wants to find a home for the dog immediately.
 C John wants the dog, but Rosa knows she cannot keep the crab.
 D Neither child wishes to have a pet.

> **Tip**
> Eliminate answer choices that are clearly false.

SCHOOL-HOME CONNECTION Talk with your child about a faraway place where a friend or a relative lives. Have your child describe two similarities and two differences between where you live and the faraway place.

40

Practice Book
On Your Mark

© Harcourt

Name _____

▶ **Read each sentence below. Then paraphrase, or sum up, the sentence in your own words.**

1. People from Maine used to trade ice for cocoa, tea, and spices.

   _____

   _____

2. Cocoa beans come from cacao pods, which grow on cacao trees.

   _____

   _____

3. When the rivers froze, men chopped blocks of ice.

   _____

   _____

   _____

4. Cream, sugar, and cocoa are poured into the can of the ice cream freezer.

   _____

5. In the morning you can see all of the ships clearly as they come in.

   _____

 SCHOOL-HOME CONNECTION Discuss a book your child has read recently. Ask your child to paraphrase a favorite section of the book.

Practice Book
On Your Mark

Name _____

Skill Reminder • A **past-tense verb** tells about action that happened in the past.
• Add **-ed** to most present-tense verbs to make them show past actions.

▶ Draw a line under the verb in each sentence. Then write whether the verb is *present tense* or *past tense*.

1. Chocolate comes from a
faraway island. _____

2. She climbed the tree early in
the morning. _____

3. Cacao trees grow only in shade. _____

4. Once, I bit a fresh cocoa bean. _____

5. We paddled along the beach. _____

▶ Complete each sentence with the correct past-tense form of the verb in parentheses ( ).

6. We finally _____ the canoe onto the beach. **(pull)**

7. We _____ the canoe in the turtle grass. **(hide)**

8. My mother _____ cocoa beans in the sun. **(dry)**

9. We _____ boiling water over the crushed beans. **(pour)**

10. Papa _____ his canoe to the river. **(drag)**

11. We _____ about the huge waves. **(worry)**

12. Fifty men _____ on the river yesterday. **(work)**

© Harcourt

Practice Book
On Your Mark

Name _____

Skill Reminder   When a word ends in a short vowel and consonant, double the consonant before you add *-ed* or *-ing*. If the word already ends in two consonants, just add *-ed* or *-ing*. If a word ends in a consonant and *e*, drop the *e* and add *-ed* or *-ing*.

▶ Fold the paper along the dotted line. As each spelling word is read aloud, write it in the blank. Then unfold your paper, and check your work. Practice spelling any words you missed.

SPELLING WORDS

1. blooming
2. settled
3. stamping
4. leaving
5. liked
6. taking
7. getting
8. filled
9. swimming
10. rolled
11. hoping
12. used
13. hurrying
14. buying
15. worried

1. _____

2. _____

3. _____

4. _____

5. _____

6. _____

7. _____

8. _____

9. _____

10. _____

11. _____

12. _____

13. _____

14. _____

15. _____

Practice Book
On Your Mark

▶ **Write the Vocabulary Word that best completes each sentence.**

congratulations	value	amount
receive	combinations	choices

1. "Did you _____ your prize yet?"

2. "Yes, I had three _____, and I chose this one."

3. "_____ on a great show."

4. "Thanks. I spent a great_____ of time practicing."

5. "There's more _____ in doing well than in winning a prize, don't you think?"

6. "Yes. It felt so good to master all the dance step_____."

▶ **Complete the sentences with a Vocabulary Word.**

7. When you pick from many items, you have

   _____.

8. When you win a game or contest, you may receive

   _____.

9. When you get something, you _____ it.

Name _____

▶ **Read the letters. Then circle the letter of the best answer to each question.**

Dear Grandma,

    Please help me explain to Mom and Dad that I am old enough to have a puppy. I take care of my pet turtle all by myself. No one has to remind me. Also, I already know a lot about puppies. I help my best friend, Ernie, take care of his puppy. I can help pay for dog food and puppy toys with my allowance.

    Mom and Dad are waiting for your letter. Thank you, Grandma!

      Love,

      Ryan

Dear Ryan,

    What a nice surprise it was to get your letter! You reminded me of your mother when she was your age. She begged for a puppy, too, until I got her one. Back then, your mother did not realize that puppies needed attention all the time. Just like you, your mother had to go to school. After school, she liked to go out and play with her friends. Guess who ended up feeding and walking your mother's puppy every day? Please write again when you have guessed.

      With much love,

      Grandma

1 Is the main idea stated in Ryan's letter?

  A Yes, in the first sentence.

  B Yes, in the second sentence.

  C Yes, in the last sentence.

  D No, the main idea is not stated.

💡 **Tip**

Most of the sentences support the main idea.

2 Is the main idea stated in Grandma's letter?

  F Yes, in the first sentence.

  G Yes, in the second sentence.

  H Yes, in the last sentence.

  J No, the main idea is not stated.

💡 **Tip**

Add up the details to identify the main idea.

© Harcourt

SCHOOL-HOME CONNECTION With your child, take turns telling what kind of pet you would like to have someday. Remind your child to support the main idea—the kind of pet—with supporting points, or details.

Practice Book
On Your Mark

▶ **Complete the test-taking strategies poster.**

Things to Do Before a Test	Things to Do During a Test
1. Be sure you know _____ _____ the test will be given.	**4.** Read all _____ _____ before you begin.
2. Get a good _____ _____ .	**5.** Answer _____ _____ first.
3. Eat _____ _____ before the test.	**6.** If there is time, _____ _____ before turning in the test.

▶ **Rewrite each test-taking tip to make it correct.**

7. Start at the beginning and answer each question in order.

_____

_____

8. Read only the first set of directions. They will work for the whole test.

_____

_____

SCHOOL-HOME CONNECTION Help your child
make a poster titled "How to Succeed at Tests." Ask
your child to use the lists he or she completed on this
page to make a list of things to do before and during a test.

46

Practice Book
On Your Mark

© Harcourt

Skill Reminder   An **irregular verb** is a verb that does not end with *-ed* in the past tense.

▶ **Draw one line under the present-tense verbs. Draw two lines under the past-tense verbs.**

1. You have one million dollars in nickels.

2. "Awesome!" your uncle says.

3. You clearly did something right.

4. He saw your stacks of nickels.

5. Now he comes to the bank with you.

▶ **Complete the sentences below. Rewrite each sentence, using the correct past-tense or present-tense form of the verb in parentheses ( ).**

6. Yesterday, a money truck _____ down the street. **(come)**

_____

7. The driver had _____ the bank. **(see)**

_____

8. He had _____, "There's the entrance." **(say)**

_____

9. Today, the money truck has _____ with more bags of cash. **(come)**

_____

10. The driver has _____ a long day. **(have)**

_____

TRY THIS!   Use past-tense forms of these verbs to write three sentences about what happened yesterday: *have, come,* and *see.*

Practice Book
On Your Mark

Name _____

Skill Reminder | Some words end with *-tion* or *-sion*, as in *station* and *version*.

▶ **Fold the paper along the dotted line. As each spelling word is read aloud, write it in the blank. Then unfold your paper, and check your work. Practice spelling any words you missed.**

1. _____

2. _____

3. _____

4. _____

5. _____

6. _____

7. _____

8. _____

9. _____

10. _____

11. _____

12. _____

13. _____

14. _____

15. _____

SPELLING WORDS

1. combination
2. action
3. vision
4. motion
5. section
6. nation
7. permission
8. confusion
9. question
10. attention
11. vacation
12. production
13. quotation
14. tension
15. sensation

Practice Book
On Your Mark

▶ **Finish the letter below. Use the Vocabulary Words to complete the sentences.**

signal	celebrations	choosy
tracks	admiring	average

Dear Grandpa,

I've been camping in the desert for a week now. It is wonderful. Just this

morning, I was **(1)** _____ the pretty flowers on the cactus plants.

Yesterday I saw two cactus plants that seemed to be reaching out to shake hands

with each other. I think they were trying to **(2)** _____ to me that the desert is really a friendly place.

Every day I see the **(3)** _____ of wild animals. Sometimes I follow them to see where they lead.

Some sunsets are just **(4)** _____, but today I saw a

special one. I am very **(5)** _____ about what I call special, as you know. The sky was red and orange and yellow.

Soon I will be home. There will be **(6)** _____ to welcome me back, I bet. Then I will tell you all about the other things I saw.

Your granddaughter,
Alicia

▶ **Write the Vocabulary Word that best completes each sentence.**

7. Animals and people leave

_____ when they walk.

8. People all around the world enjoy _____.

Practice Book
On Your Mark

Name _____

▶ **Read the paragraph. Then circle the letter of the best answer to each question.**

People all over the world celebrate birthdays. In Scotland, a special cake is baked with a coin inside for some lucky guest to find. Children in Guatemala often play a birthday game. Blindfolded players take turns trying to hit a piñata filled with coins and candy. When the piñata breaks, everybody runs to catch the coins and candy. No matter how they are celebrated, birthdays are fun.

1 Which phrase best describes the topic of the paragraph?

   A playing games   **C** birthday celebrations

   B birthday game   **D** coins and candy

> 💡 **Tip**
>
> Remember that the main topic is the focus of every sentence in the paragraph.

2 Which idea belongs in a summary of the paragraph?

   F Children love cake and ice cream.

   G A slice of Scottish birthday cake might have a coin in it.

   H Birthday parties without games are not fun.

   J A piñata is hard to break.

> 💡 **Tip**
>
> A good summary tells about the main ideas from the paragraph. It does not include other ideas or information.

3 Which question can best help you summarize the paragraph?

   A What else do I know about this topic?

   B What is my opinion about this topic?

   C What idea or topic do all of the details tell about?

   D Why did the author decide to write about this topic?

> 💡 **Tip**
>
> Remember that a summary retells only what you have read. It does not include other information.

SCHOOL-HOME CONNECTION With your child, discuss how you celebrate important events. Then ask your child to write a summary about one family celebration you discussed.

50

Practice Book
On Your Mark

© Harcourt

Skill Reminder   An **irregular verb** is a verb that does not end with *-ed* to show past tense.

▶ **Rewrite each sentence. Change present-tense verbs to past tense. Change past-tense verbs to present tense.**

1. I give each day a name.

_____

2. Today I rode in a pickup truck.

_____

3. Seven dust devils went by.

_____

4. I take pictures of the dust devils.

_____

5. I write about special days in my journal.

_____

▶ **Complete each sentence with the correct past-tense form of the verb in parentheses ( ).**

6. Later, I _____ down to the canyon. **(go)**

7. I always _____ a sketchpad with me. **(take)**

8. Once, I had _____ a picture of a hawk. **(take)**

9. The hawk had _____ on the wind. **(ride)**

10. Then it _____ something in the field. **(eat)**

TRY THIS! Write three sentences about a place you like to visit. Use past-tense forms of the verbs *go*, *ride*, and *take*.

© Harcourt

Name _____

Skill Reminder   Some words end with the suffixes *-er,* *-ful, -ly,* or *-able,* such as *rancher, helpful, loudly,* and *singable.*

▶ Fold the paper along the dotted line. As each spelling word is read aloud, write it in the blank. Then unfold your paper, and check your work. Practice spelling any words you missed.

1. _____

2. _____

3. _____

4. _____

5. _____

6. _____

7. _____

8. _____

9. _____

10. _____

11. _____

12. _____

13. _____

14. _____

15. _____

16. _____

SPELLING WORDS

1. farmer
2. useful
3. softly
4. suitable
5. lonely
6. quietly
7. teacher
8. thankful
9. exactly
10. readable
11. nicer
12. safer
13. harmful
14. playful
15. quietly
16. suddenly

© Harcourt

Practice Book
On Your Mark

▶ On the line next to each clue, write the Vocabulary Word that answers the question.

| windmill | cherished | furrows |
| ample | shunned | growth |

1. We are long grooves cut by a plow in the ground. What are we?

_____

2. We are a group of plants growing in a certain area. What are we?

_____

3. I am a machine powered by wind. What am I?

_____

4. I am always more than enough. What am I?

_____

5. I would feel sad if you did this to me.

_____

6. It would be wonderful if I always felt this way.

_____

Name _____

▶ **Read the poster. Suppose that you are visiting a wildlife park. What animals might you see? In the chart below, write three causes and their effects if you offered food to some animals you saw during your visit.**

Why You Should Not Feed Wild Animals

1. Finding food is a natural survival skill for wild animals. When you feed wild animals, they may expect to be fed and stop looking for the food they need to live.

2. Many large wild animals, such as deer and bighorn sheep, have stomachs designed for a diet of grass and shrubs. When you feed them cookies and other junk food, they may have trouble digesting the new food and may even get sick.

3. Wild animals that get used to being fed can be dangerous. When a large bear comes charging toward your car on a trip to a wildlife park, remember: people have probably been feeding that poor bear.

Cause	Effect
1.	
2.	
3.	

© Harcourt

▶ **Read the story. Then circle the letter of the best answer to each question.**

Hattie has the best garden I have seen. Her first garden, though, was a mess because she didn't know some important rules. She planted the seeds under a thin layer of soil. When it rained, the top layer of soil washed away. As a result, birds saw the seeds and ate them. Then Hattie watered the aloe plants too much, since she thought that plants always need water. After her last aloe plant was destroyed, Hattie decided to go straight to the Green Thumb Bookstore. In order to avoid more mistakes, she read a book called *How to Grow a Great Garden.*

1 Which statement sums up why Hattie's first garden failed?

A She did not dig deep enough to plant the seeds.

B She did not know some important gardening rules.

C She did not read a gardening book before she started.

D She watered her aloe plants too much.

> 💡 **Tip**
> Which statement sums up *all* of the reasons that Hattie's garden failed?

2 What did Hattie learn about planting when birds ate the seeds?

F to cover the soil to protect seeds from the rain

G to keep birds away from the garden

H to plant seeds deeper in the ground

J to read about gardening before planting

> 💡 **Tip**
> Think about what the question asks: What did *Hattie learn about planting?*

3 What finally caused Hattie to go to the bookstore?

A Her last aloe plant was destroyed.

B Her garden was a muddy mess.

C She wanted a gardening book.

D The top layer of soil washed away.

> 💡 **Tip**
> What single event finally made Hattie decide to go to the bookstore?

SCHOOL-HOME CONNECTION With your child, write and illustrate a how-to poster about something he or she knows how to do. Make each sentence a cause-and-effect statement, using signal words such as *because, therefore, in order to, as a result,* and *since.*

55

Skill Reminder • Forms of the verb *be* link the subject
of a sentence to the predicate.
• **The subject of the sentence and the form of *be* must agree.
When the subject is one person or thing, use *am, is,* or *was*.
When the subject is more than one, use *are* or *were*.**

▶ Underline the forms of the verb *be*. Write whether each is *present* or
past tense.

1. Alejandro was a kind man. _____

2. The animals were pleased with his gift. _____

3. Now he is less lonely. _____

4. The animals are happier, too. _____

5. I am glad for all of them. _____

▶ Rewrite each sentence, using the form of *be* given in parentheses ( ).

6. You _____ rarely alone. **(present)**

_____

7. He _____ with his friends. **(present)**

_____

8. I _____ a friendly person. **(present)**

_____

9. He _____ lonely for his family. **(past)**

_____

10. They _____ far away. **(present)**

_____

Practice Book
On Your Mark

Name _____

Skill Reminder   When a word ends in a consonant and
y, change y to i before adding -es or -ed: *fairies, hurried.*

▶ Fold the paper along the dotted line. As each
spelling word is read aloud, write it in the
blank. Then unfold your paper, and check your
work. Practice spelling any words you missed.

1. _____

2. _____

3. _____

4. _____

5. _____

6. _____

7. _____

8. _____

9. _____

10. _____

11. _____

12. _____

13. _____

14. _____

15. _____

SPELLING WORDS

1. pennies
2. buried
3. replied
4. candies
5. emptied
6. stories
7. married
8. copies
9. parties
10. studied
11. mysteries
12. discoveries
13. worries
14. families
15. ponies

Practice Book
On Your Mark

Name _____

▶ **Write the Vocabulary Word that answers each riddle.**

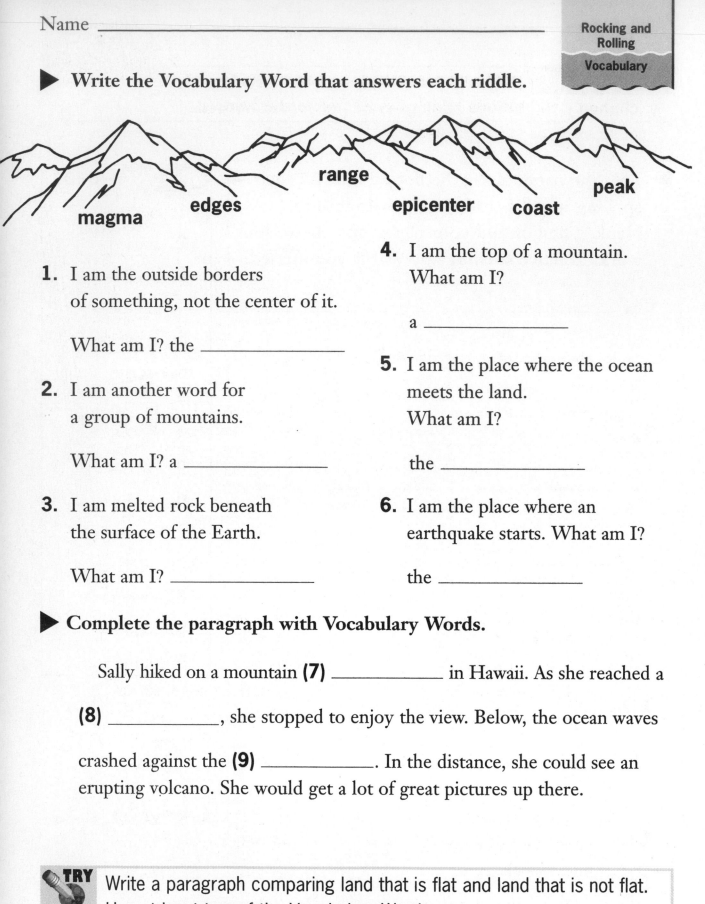

range

edges   **epicenter**   **coast**   **peak**

magma

1. I am the outside borders
of something, not the center of it.

What am I? the _____

2. I am another word for
a group of mountains.

What am I? a _____

3. I am melted rock beneath
the surface of the Earth.

What am I? _____

4. I am the top of a mountain.
What am I?

a _____

5. I am the place where the ocean
meets the land.
What am I?

the _____

6. I am the place where an
earthquake starts. What am I?

the _____

▶ **Complete the paragraph with Vocabulary Words.**

Sally hiked on a mountain **(7)** _____ in Hawaii. As she reached a

(8) _____, she stopped to enjoy the view. Below, the ocean waves

crashed against the **(9)** _____. In the distance, she could see an
erupting volcano. She would get a lot of great pictures up there.

TRY THIS! Write a paragraph comparing land that is flat and land that is not flat.
Use at least two of the Vocabulary Words.

© Harcourt

58

► Which pair of guide words would appear at the top of
the page that contains each word? Circle the letter of
the answer to each question.

EARTH

EASTERN

1 earthquake

   A earth—eastern

   B element—elevation

   C emanate—equation

   D equator—Everest

2 epicenter

   F earth—eastern

   G element—elevation

   H emanate—equation

   J equator—Everest

3 erosion

   A earth—eastern

   B element—elevation

   C emanate—equation

   D equator—Everest

4 environment

   F earth—eastern

   G element—elevation

   H emanate—equation

   J equator—Everest

5 elementary

   A earth—eastern

   B element—elevation

   C emanate—equation

   D equator—Everest

6 equinox

   F earth—eastern

   G element—elevation

   H emanate—equation

   J equator—Everest

▶ **Read the paragraph below. Then circle the letter of the best answer to each question.**

> I am writing a paper about how the crust of the Earth changes over time. First, I will research the different layers of the Earth. I want to find out how the core causes the surface to change shape. I need to look up some terms, too. For example, I don't know what *magma* means. My teacher, Mrs. Globetrotter, says that I should find the information I need in books that were written recently. She says scientists are always finding out new things and changing the facts. She even told me that scientists once thought the Earth was flat!

1 In which part of a book about earth science could you find the starting page of a chapter?

  A copyright page   **C** index

  B glossary   **D** table of contents

> 💡 **Tip**
> Where do you find chapter titles listed in order?

2 In which part of a book could you find out what the word *magma* means?

  F copyright page   **H** index

  G glossary   **J** table of contents

> 💡 **Tip**
> Think about where you would find both the word *and* its definition.

3 In which part of the book could you find out the date it was published?

  A copyright page   **C** index

  B glossary   **D** table of contents

> 💡 **Tip**
> Ignore the answers you know are wrong.

SCHOOL-HOME CONNECTION With your child, examine the different parts of a nonfiction book. Look at the copyright page. Try out the index by turning to pages listed for a topic your child chooses. Look at the table of contents and guess the main ideas of the book.

Practice Book
On Your Mark

▶ **Study the following bar graph. Then answer the questions below.**

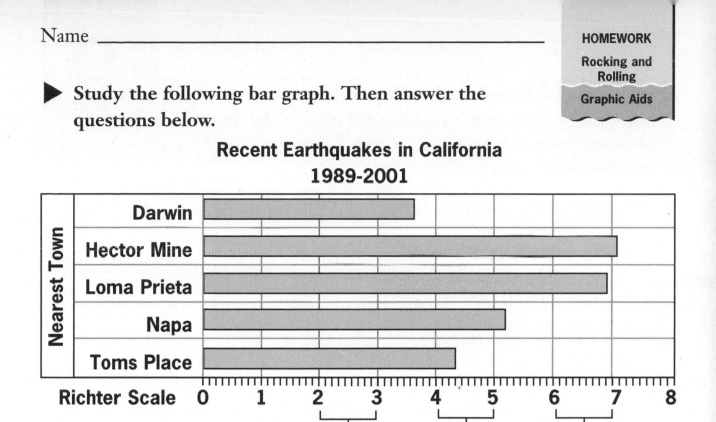

Recent Earthquakes in California
1989-2001

1. Where did the two biggest earthquakes take place?

   _____

2. What damage may have occurred from the earthquake in Loma Prieta?

   _____

3. Where in the United States did all of these earthquakes take place?

   _____

4. About how many points of difference is there between the earthquake

   near Darwin and the one near Hector? _____

SCHOOL-HOME CONNECTION With your child, write the exact magnitude on the Richter Scale of two earthquakes recorded on the graph. Talk about how each earthquake might have felt and the kinds of damage it may have caused.

Practice Book
On Your Mark

Name _____

Skill Reminder • A **contraction** is a short way to write
two words. An apostrophe (') takes the place of the missing
letter or letters. The two words, usually a pronoun and a form of the
verbs *be* and *do*, are joined together.

▶ **Write the two words that make up each contraction.**

1. We're studying earth science in school.   _____

2. Isn't the Earth always changing?   _____

3. I don't think earth science is boring at all!   _____

4. It's fun to study volcanoes.   _____

5. Aren't earthquakes scary and exciting?   _____

▶ **Rewrite each sentence using a contraction**
in place of the underlined words.

6. <u>What is</u> the highest mountain range?

_____

7. <u>That is</u> the subject of my next science project.

_____

8. The Rockies <u>are not</u> the oldest mountains in the United States.

_____

9. <u>We are</u> going camping near a volcano next summer.

_____

10. <u>I am</u> planning to hike all the way around the rim.

_____

**TRY
THIS!** Write contractions for *would not* and *it is*. Use your contractions in a
journal paragraph. Describe what it may be like to be near an earthquake.

Practice Book
On Your Mark

Name _____

Skill Reminder   A **contraction** is a short way to say
and write two words. An **apostrophe** replaces any missing letters.

► Fold the paper along the dotted line. As each
spelling word is read aloud, write it in the
blank. Then unfold your paper, and check
your work. Practice spelling any words
you missed.

1. _____

2. _____

3. _____

4. _____

5. _____

6. _____

7. _____

8. _____

9. _____

10. _____

11. _____

12. _____

13. _____

14. _____

15. _____

SPELLING WORDS

1. it's
2. isn't
3. you've
4. we'd
5. didn't
6. she's
7. we've
8. haven't
9. he'd
10. they'd
11. there's
12. don't
13. we'll
14. won't
15. he's

© Harcourt

63

Name _____

▶ **Write the Vocabulary Word that belongs in each group.**

eventually	converse	continent
universe	homeward	sphere

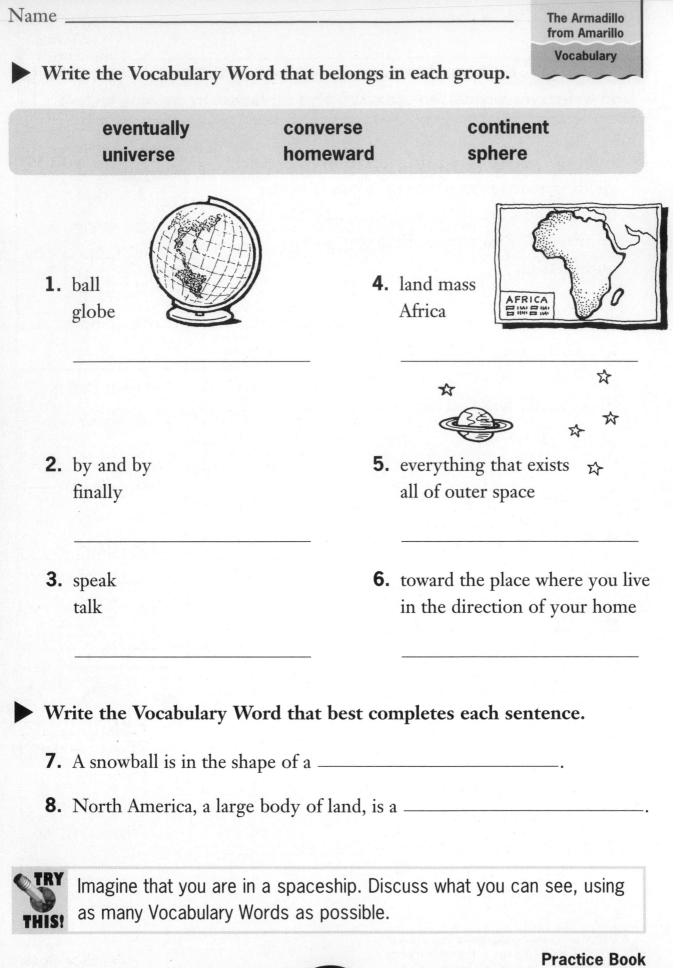

1. ball
globe

_____

2. by and by
finally

_____

3. speak
talk

_____

4. land mass
Africa

_____

5. everything that exists
all of outer space

_____

6. toward the place where you live
in the direction of your home

_____

▶ **Write the Vocabulary Word that best completes each sentence.**

7. A snowball is in the shape of a _____.

8. North America, a large body of land, is a _____.

TRY THIS! Imagine that you are in a spaceship. Discuss what you can see, using as many Vocabulary Words as possible.

Practice Book
On Your Mark

Name _____

► **Read the paragraph. Then circle the letter of the best answer to each question below.**

The national symbol of the United States is the bald eagle. The law protects bald eagles from being hunted by people. Also, eagles build their nests high in trees or on rocky ledges so that animals cannot reach them. However, bald eagles are still in danger of disappearing. Eagles are hurt by the sprays farmers use to keep insects off food plants. The sprays, called pesticides, can cause eggshells to break. The number of bald eagles born has dropped very low.

1 What caused the bald eagle to be in danger of disappearing?
   A being the national symbol of the United States
   B building nests on rocky ledges
   C the use of pesticides
   D being helpless when newly hatched

💡 **Tip**
Eliminate the answer that is not dangerous. Rate the remaining answers by how dangerous they are.

2 What effect does the author say pesticides have on eggs?
   F They make the birds hatch sooner.
   G They make the eggshells weaker.
   H They make newborn birds smaller.
   J They make the shells stronger.

💡 **Tip**
Look for signal words, such as *cause*.

3 How does building a high nest help the eagle survive?
   A Young eagles learn to fly by falling out of the nest.
   B Pesticides are not sprayed that high.
   C Animals can easily eat the eagle eggs.
   D Animals can't reach the eagles' nests.

💡 **Tip**
Look for the effect signaled by the words *so that*.

© Harcourt

SCHOOL-HOME CONNECTION With your child, brainstorm and list events or activities in daily life that involve cause and effect. Together, make a cause-and-effect chart that you can fill in.

Practice Book
On Your Mark

Name _____

Skill Reminder • An **adverb** is a word that describes a verb.
• An adverb may tell *how, when,* or *where.*

▶ **Underline the verb. Circle the adverb that describes it.**

1. The armadillo lands shakily.

2. He sits down with a sigh.

3. The eagle flaps his beautiful wings again.

4. The armadillo waves sleepily.

5. Then he closes his eyes.

▶ **Write what each underlined adverb tells:**
where, when, or *how.*

6. Together we fly into the sky. _____

7. We see all of Texas below. _____

8. Now I can see Mexico. _____

9. It shines brightly in the sun. _____

10. We return to Earth afterward._____

▶ **Choose two sentences from 1–10. Rewrite each sentence, using a different adverb.**

11. _____

_____

12. _____

_____

Practice Book
On Your Mark

Name _____

Skill Reminder   The ending sound you hear in *ever* is usually spelled *er*.

▶ Fold the paper along the dotted line. As each spelling word is read aloud, write it in the blank. Then unfold your paper, and check your work. Practice spelling any words you missed.

1. _____

2. _____

3. _____

4. _____

5. _____

6. _____

7. _____

8. _____

9. _____

10. _____

11. _____

12. _____

13. _____

14. _____

15. _____

SPELLING WORDS

1. water
2. over
3. never
4. under
5. river
6. number
7. wonder
8. tower
9. rather
10. finger
11. center
12. prefer
13. better
14. border
15. fever

67

Practice Book
On Your Mark

Name _____

▶ **Write the Vocabulary Word that best completes each analogy.**

| force | nucleus | loops |
| solar wind | particles | fluorescent |

1. *Astronomy* is to *science* as *gravity* is to _____.

2. *Seed* is to *fruit* as _____ is to *comet*.

3. *Zigzags* are to *roller coasters* as _____ are to *ferris wheels*.

4. *Tiny* is to *huge* as _____ are to *comets*.

5. *Light* is to _____ as *sound* is to *musical*.

6. *Moonlight* is to *moon* as _____ is to *sun*.

▶ **Write a Vocabulary Word to complete each rhyme.**

7. I sang with such _____
   That I soon became hoarse.

8. The scientist wrote articles

   About ice _____.

9. Elliptical _____
   Move like hula hoops.

TRY THIS! Make up riddles for at least two Vocabulary Words. For example: I am strong. I can move things. What am I? (force)

Practice Book
On Your Mark

© Harcourt

Name _____

▶ **Suppose you are reading a book about outer space. Choose which part of the book you would use to find the answer to each question. Circle the letter of the answer you have chosen.**

1 On what page does the chapter titled "Comets" begin?

   A glossary

   B index

   C table of contents

   D title page

💡 **Tip**

Ignore the answer choices you know are wrong.

2 What is the meaning of *gravity*?

   F glossary

   G index

   H table of contents

   J title page

💡 **Tip**

Where do you look up definitions?

3 On what pages is the astronomer Jan H. Oort mentioned?

   A glossary

   B index

   C table of contents

   D title page

💡 **Tip**

Where can you find a list of names and page numbers?

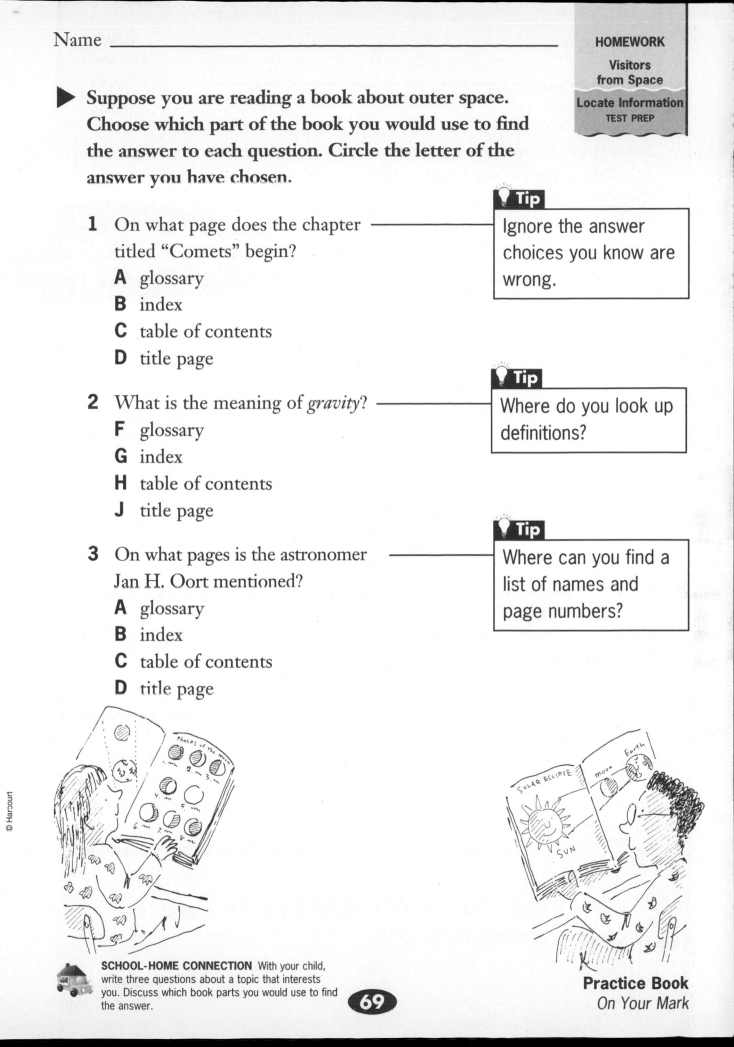

© Harcourt

SCHOOL-HOME CONNECTION With your child, write three questions about a topic that interests you. Discuss which book parts you would use to find the answer.

Practice Book
On Your Mark

Name _____

Skill Reminder   • You can use **adverbs** to compare two
or more actions.
• Use either **-er** or *more* with adverbs to compare two actions.
• Use either **-est** or *most* with adverbs to compare more than two
actions.

▶ **Rewrite each sentence, using the correct
adverb in parentheses ( ).**

1. Does a comet burn **(hotter, hottest)** than a star?

_____

2. A comet moves **(more quickly, most quickly)** than an asteroid.

_____

3. Do comets glow **(more brightly, most brightly)** than the moon?

_____

▶ **Fill in the blank, using the correct form of the adverb in parentheses ( ).**

4. The comet burned _____ than a wildfire.
(steadily)

5. It glowed the _____ of all the objects. **(clearly)**

6. It appeared _____ than the moon. **(high)**

7. It moved _____ than a planet would. **(quick)**

8. It burned _____ of all the comets seen. **(longest)**

 TRY THIS!   Use *fast, faster,* and *fastest* in three sentences comparing three
comets. Give the comets names.

© Harcourt

Practice Book
On Your Mark

Skill Reminder The ending sound you hear in *little* and
petal can be spelled *le* or *al*.

▶ Fold the paper along the dotted line. As each
spelling word is read aloud, write it in the
blank. Then unfold your paper, and check your
work. Practice spelling any words you missed.

1. _____

2. _____

3. _____

4. _____

5. _____

6. _____

7. _____

8. _____

9. _____

10. _____

11. _____

12. _____

13. _____

14. _____

15. _____

SPELLING WORDS

1. simple
2. total
3. applc
4. title
5. central
6. purple
7. signal
8. normal
9. middle
10. able
11. terrible
12. people
13. medal
14. handle
15. single

Skills and Strategies Index

COMPREHENSION

GRAMMAR

LITERARY RESPONSE AND ANALYSIS

SPELLING

RESEARCH AND INFORMATION

VOCABULARY

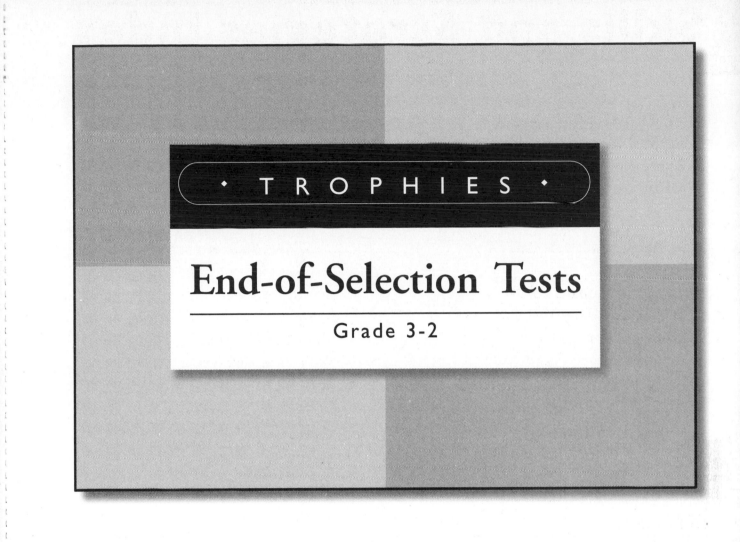

End-of-Selection Tests

Grade 3-2

Papa Tells Chita a Story

Grade 3-2

Directions: For items 1–18, fill in the circle in front of the correct answer. For questions 19–20, write the answer.

Vocabulary

1. Picking fresh blackberries is fun until you get scratched and cut from the _____.
Ⓐ stumbling   Ⓑ brambles
Ⓒ weary   Ⓓ colonel

2. The _____ commanded his troops to march into battle.
Ⓐ colonel   Ⓑ urgent
Ⓒ soldier   Ⓓ weary

3. Everyone cheered when a _____ marched down the street in the parade.
Ⓐ stumbling   Ⓑ brambles
Ⓒ soldier   Ⓓ smart

4. We were _____ after a long day of testing in class.
Ⓐ weary   Ⓑ stumbling
Ⓒ urgent   Ⓓ soldier

5. Dad's arms were _____ to show he wanted a hug.
Ⓐ weary   Ⓑ urgent
Ⓒ outstretched   Ⓓ stumbling

6. The tired boys were _____ down the rocky trail.
Ⓐ urgent   Ⓑ outstretched
Ⓒ brambles   Ⓓ stumbling

7. When he fell and broke his arm, he needed _____ medical care.

Ⓐ weary   Ⓑ urgent

Ⓒ outstretched   Ⓓ colonel

Comprehension

8. Chita likes her special time with Papa because she _____ .

Ⓐ gets out of doing the dishes

Ⓑ can help Papa in his office

Ⓒ likes the stories Papa tells

Ⓓ tells Mama to hurry with the dishes

9. Papa works as a _____ .

Ⓐ doctor   Ⓑ cowboy

Ⓒ storyteller   Ⓓ teacher

10. In this story, Papa fights in _____ .

Ⓐ the American War   Ⓑ the Civil War

Ⓒ World War II   Ⓓ the Spanish War

11. Chita knows so much about Papa's story ahead of time because she has _____ .

Ⓐ read ahead of him   Ⓑ seen it before

Ⓒ heard it many times   Ⓓ read it before

12. Where does Papa's story take place?

Ⓐ Mexico   Ⓑ Cuba

Ⓒ United States   Ⓓ Africa

Practice Book
On Your Mark

13. In Papa's story, the problem for the colonel is he didn't have enough _____ .

   Ⓐ weapons and supplies   Ⓑ supplies and medicine

   Ⓒ soldiers and supplies   Ⓓ soldiers and pouches

14. The colonel's problem is solved because Papa volunteers to _____ .

   Ⓐ take a secret letter to the other troops

   Ⓑ find the materials in the swamp on his own

   Ⓒ use his knowledge to make supplies

   Ⓓ swim with alligators to prove he is brave

15. Papa convinced the colonel that he was the _____ soldier.

   Ⓐ strongest   Ⓑ fastest

   Ⓒ smartest   Ⓓ bravest

16. Majestic was a _____ .

   Ⓐ soldier   Ⓑ horse

   Ⓒ snake   Ⓓ bird

17. Papa probably had a pouch made of oilskin in the story because oilskin is _____ .

   Ⓐ pretty   Ⓑ hard

   Ⓒ waterproof   Ⓓ old

18. In the story Papa tells, where does he try to sleep that night?

   Ⓐ close to the water   Ⓑ in the swamp

   Ⓒ on the high hill   Ⓓ in an eagle's nest

19. Tell what the officer in charge does when Papa finally arrives with his message.

_____

_____

_____

_____

_____

_____

_____

20. Why could this story be called a tall tale?

_____

_____

_____

_____

_____

_____

_____

Practice Book
On Your Mark

Coyote Places the Stars

Directions: For items 1–18, fill in the circle in front of the correct answer. For items 19–20, write the answer.

Vocabulary

1. The sides of the _____ were steep.
- Ⓐ feast
- Ⓑ swiftly
- Ⓒ canyon
- Ⓓ pride

2. We couldn't stop _____ at the little red-headed girl because she was so cute.
- Ⓐ gazing
- Ⓑ skillful
- Ⓒ swiftly
- Ⓓ arranged

3. Ed is very _____ at drawing pictures of horses.
- Ⓐ pride
- Ⓑ skillful
- Ⓒ arranged
- Ⓓ swiftly

4. The little children _____ the blocks in the shape of a house.
- Ⓐ gazing
- Ⓑ pride
- Ⓒ arranged
- Ⓓ skillful

5. Jan ran so _____ in the race that she finished in first place.
- Ⓐ arranged
- Ⓑ pride
- Ⓒ swiftly
- Ⓓ feast

6. Tina took _____ in her many accomplishments.
- Ⓐ pride
- Ⓑ gazing
- Ⓒ canyon
- Ⓓ arranged

7. Our family has a _____ every Thanksgiving Day.
Ⓐ pride   Ⓑ swiftly
Ⓒ feast   Ⓓ canyon

Comprehension

8. This story is most like a _____ .
Ⓐ tall tale   Ⓑ fairy tale
Ⓒ riddle   Ⓓ legend

9. When does this story take place?
Ⓐ during a full moon   Ⓑ after a bad storm
Ⓒ recently   Ⓓ many years in the past

10. Coyote shoots one arrow after the other at the sky because he _____ .
Ⓐ is practicing his shooting
Ⓑ is showing off for Bear
Ⓒ is connecting arrows to make a ladder
Ⓓ can't carry arrows to the moon

11. Which event happens first?
Ⓐ Coyote makes a picture of Bear from stars.
Ⓑ Coyote begins to howl.
Ⓒ Coyote returns to Earth.
Ⓓ Coyote hits a star with an arrow and makes it move.

Practice Book
On Your Mark

Grade 3-2

12. Where does Coyote get his ideas for most of the star pictures he draws?

Ⓐ by thinking about himself and his friends

Ⓑ from the stars

Ⓒ from ideas that Bear gives him

Ⓓ by looking at shapes on the moon

13. To the other animals in the story, Coyote's howl is _____ .

Ⓐ cruel Ⓑ angry

Ⓒ unhappy Ⓓ mysterious

14. Which group do the words whoofing, whiffing, screeching, and squawking belong to?

Ⓐ ways arrows may fly Ⓑ dives that birds make

Ⓒ sounds animals make Ⓓ things that Coyote does

15. According to the story, Coyote makes animal-shaped pictures because _____ .

Ⓐ they are the easiest to make

Ⓑ stargazers in the future will think of the animals

Ⓒ all the animals vote for them

Ⓓ the moon orders him to

16. The animals give a great feast because _____ .

Ⓐ they want to honor Coyote

Ⓑ it is the end of the summer

Ⓒ they are all hungry

Ⓓ Eagle tells them to do so

17. Which word best tells about Coyote?

Ⓐ dangerous Ⓑ musical

Ⓒ fearful Ⓓ imaginative

Practice Book
On Your Mark

18. What is the purpose of this story?

Ⓐ to give facts about coyotes

Ⓑ to explain the appearance of the night sky

Ⓒ to tell how to shoot a bow and arrow

Ⓓ to describe desert animals

19. Name two things that show how clever Coyote is.

_____

_____

_____

_____

_____

_____

20. "Rabbits hippity-hopped" when they went to see Coyote. List three other animals in the story and tell how each moved.

_____

_____

_____

_____

_____

_____

_____

_____

Why Mosquitoes Buzz in People's Ears

Directions: For items 1–18, fill in the circle in front of the correct answer. For items 19–20, write the answer.

Vocabulary

1. Everything he said is _____ because the facts in the case make no sense.
  Ⓐ nonsense   Ⓑ tidbit
  Ⓒ council   Ⓓ mischief

2. The little boy has a silly grin on his face, so he may be up to some _____ .
  Ⓐ duty   Ⓑ satisfied
  Ⓒ mischief   Ⓓ tidbit

3. It is the children's _____ to follow school rules.
  Ⓐ satisfied   Ⓑ council
  Ⓒ mischief   Ⓓ duty

4. The _____ voted in favor of building a new school.
  Ⓐ council   Ⓑ tidbit
  Ⓒ nonsense   Ⓓ mischief

5. Are you _____ with the story you are writing?
  Ⓐ satisfied   Ⓑ council
  Ⓒ duty   Ⓓ nonsense

6. There is only a _____ of meat left in the pan.
  Ⓐ council   Ⓑ satisfied
  Ⓒ mischief   Ⓓ tidbit

Practice Book
On Your Mark

Comprehension

7. In this selection, a <u>yam</u> is a _____ .

Ⓐ white potato   Ⓑ sweet potato

Ⓒ turnip   Ⓓ weed

8. Why does the iguana think that the mosquito's story is nonsense?

Ⓐ Yams are always smaller than mosquitoes.

Ⓑ Yams and mosquitoes are the same size.

Ⓒ Mosquitoes are tiny compared to yams.

Ⓓ There is no such thing as a yam.

9. The iguana puts sticks in his ears because _____ .

Ⓐ he doesn't want to hear what the mosquito is saying

Ⓑ he is trying to be funny

Ⓒ the mosquito is talking too loudly and too fast

Ⓓ the mosquito is buzzing around in his ears

10. The iguana "went off, mek, mek, mek." In the story, the words <u>mek</u> and <u>krik</u> are _____ .

Ⓐ the different things animals smell

Ⓑ how the animals sound as they move

Ⓒ how things taste

Ⓓ what the animals see

11. Who warns the other animals of danger?

Ⓐ the mosquito and the iguana

Ⓑ the python and the rabbit

Ⓒ the crow and the monkey

Ⓓ King Lion and the owl

Practice Book
On Your Mark

12. The monkey leaps "kili wili through the trees." In this story, <u>kili</u> <u>wili</u> means _____ .

Ⓐ easily   Ⓑ calmly

Ⓒ excitedly   Ⓓ quietly

13. How does King Lion find out why the sun is still sleeping?

Ⓐ He asks the owlets.

Ⓑ He searches for the mosquito, who is hiding.

Ⓒ He brings the mosquito before the council.

Ⓓ He asks each animal what has happened.

14. The iguana doesn't speak to the python because the iguana _____ .

Ⓐ is mad at the snake

Ⓑ is planning some mischief

Ⓒ is in a hurry

Ⓓ can't hear with sticks in his ears

15. The author repeated some lines in this story to make the _____ .

Ⓐ story easier to read

Ⓑ story longer

Ⓒ story fun to read

Ⓓ story difficult to read

16. Which sentence best tells about the mosquito?

Ⓐ She still whines in people's ears.

Ⓑ She tries to do good for others.

Ⓒ She causes trouble on purpose.

Ⓓ She is very brave.

Grade 3-2

17. At the end of the story, what does <u>KPAO</u>! stand for?

  Ⓐ the sound of someone shouting

  Ⓑ the sound of someone slapping at a mosquito

  Ⓒ a word meaning "yes"

  Ⓓ the sound of a mosquito buzzing

18. "Coyote Places the Stars" and "Why Mosquitoes Buzz in People's Ears" are similar because both stories _____ .

  Ⓐ are about real animals and are factual

  Ⓑ have animal characters and explain about something in nature

  Ⓒ are humorous and have nonsense verses

  Ⓓ are like a science textbook

19. How does Mother Owl wake the sun?

_____

_____

_____

_____

20. Why do mosquitoes buzz in people's ears?

_____

_____

_____

_____

Practice Book
On Your Mark

Lon Po Po

Grade 3-2

Directions: For items 1–18, fill in the circle in front of the correct answer. For items 19–20, write the answer.

Vocabulary

1. Please _____ the gate on your way out.
   - Ⓐ tender
   - Ⓑ brittle
   - Ⓒ latch
   - Ⓓ dusk

2. Grandfather's hard bones had become _____ as he got older.
   - Ⓐ embraced
   - Ⓑ delighted
   - Ⓒ brittle
   - Ⓓ cunning

3. The time of day between daylight and nighttime is called _____ .
   - Ⓐ dusk
   - Ⓑ tender
   - Ⓒ latch
   - Ⓓ brittle

4. In many stories a fox is shown as sly and _____ .
   - Ⓐ tender
   - Ⓑ embraced
   - Ⓒ brittle
   - Ⓓ cunning

5. Dad was _____ when I showed him my good grades.
   - Ⓐ delighted
   - Ⓑ brittle
   - Ⓒ embraced
   - Ⓓ dusk

6. Mom and Dad _____ me when I arrived home from camp.
   - Ⓐ latch
   - Ⓑ tender
   - Ⓒ embraced
   - Ⓓ cunning

Grade 3-2

7. I did not need to use my knife to cut the meat because it was so _____ .

  Ⓐ delighted   Ⓑ tender

  Ⓒ embraced   Ⓓ cunning

Comprehension

8. <u>Po Po</u> is the Chinese word for _____ .

  Ⓐ wolf   Ⓑ poor

  Ⓒ grandmother   Ⓓ daughter

9. Mother leaves the children alone in the house because _____ .

  Ⓐ she is going to visit Grandmother on her birthday

  Ⓑ the children have school in the morning

  Ⓒ it is too far for the children to walk to Grandmother's house

  Ⓓ the children are busy making dinner

10. The wolf disguises himself as an old woman so he can _____ .

  Ⓐ make the children think he needs a bed for the night

  Ⓑ fool the children into thinking he is Po Po

  Ⓒ call the children his little jewels

  Ⓓ make the children think their mother came home early

11. When the wolf says "All the chicks are in the coop," he is telling the children it is time to _____ .

  Ⓐ sleep   Ⓑ eat

  Ⓒ work   Ⓓ hide

12. Who discovers that the old woman is really a wolf?

  Ⓐ Mother   Ⓑ Po Po

  Ⓒ Shang   Ⓓ Tao

Practice Book
On Your Mark

13. The eldest child figures out how to get away from the wolf by _____ .

Ⓐ reminding him that she has not latched the door
Ⓑ convincing him that children do not make a good meal
Ⓒ telling him that she will go outside and find him some food
Ⓓ complaining that she is cold and must find another blanket

14. Gingko nuts grow on _____ .

Ⓐ a tall tree   Ⓑ the ground
Ⓒ a bush   Ⓓ a tall vine

15. Shang gets the wolf in the basket by telling him he must _____ .

Ⓐ put the chickens back into the coop before he eats them
Ⓑ pluck the gingko nuts himself for the magic to work
Ⓒ help all three children out of a very tall tree
Ⓓ gather firewood before dinner can be cooked

16. The wolf said he could not climb the tree because he was too _____ .

Ⓐ stubborn   Ⓑ lazy
Ⓒ mean   Ⓓ frail

17. In this story, "the wolf's heart broke to pieces" means that the wolf _____ .

Ⓐ became sad
Ⓑ splintered his heart into pieces
Ⓒ died
Ⓓ had a heart attack

Practice Book
On Your Mark

18. This story is most like a _____ .

Ⓐ riddle

Ⓑ fable

Ⓒ legend

Ⓓ folktale

19. Name one way Shang talks the wolf into wanting gingko nuts.

_____

_____

_____

_____

_____

20. Describe how Shang gets rid of the wolf.

_____

_____

_____

_____

_____

_____

_____

_____

Practice Book
On Your Mark

Grade 3-2

The Crowded House

Directions: For items 1–18, fill in the circle in front of the correct answer. For items 19–20, write the answer.

Vocabulary

1. This cold weather is the most _____ weather we have had in years!
- Ⓐ dreadful
- Ⓑ wailing
- Ⓒ faring
- Ⓓ advice

2. That loud noise scared me out of my _____ !
- Ⓐ wits
- Ⓑ dreadful
- Ⓒ advice
- Ⓓ farewell

3. The baby's _____ in the other room let us know he was hungry.
- Ⓐ dreadful
- Ⓑ wits
- Ⓒ wailing
- Ⓓ advice

4. Please give me some _____ on how to solve this problem.
- Ⓐ farewell
- Ⓑ advice
- Ⓒ dreadful
- Ⓓ faring

5. Will she bid us _____ as she is leaving?
- Ⓐ faring
- Ⓑ wailing
- Ⓒ farewell
- Ⓓ dreadful

6. We were _____ well, despite the freezing temperatures.
- Ⓐ wailing
- Ⓑ advice
- Ⓒ dreadful
- Ⓓ faring

Grade 3-2

Practice Book
On Your Mark

Grade 3-2

Comprehension

7. This story is most like a _____ .

Ⓐ mystery   Ⓑ myth

Ⓒ biography   Ⓓ folktale

8. When does this story take place?

Ⓐ past   Ⓑ present

Ⓒ forever   Ⓓ future

9. Where does this play take place?

Ⓐ in a crowded school

Ⓑ in a carpenter's cottage

Ⓒ in the countryside

Ⓓ in Granny's cabin

10. Why do family members seem to be in each other's way?

Ⓐ The cottage has only one room.

Ⓑ Bartholomew came to visit.

Ⓒ No one moves out of the goat's way.

Ⓓ Everyone is playing in the cottage.

11. How do the family members get along with one another?

Ⓐ They are polite and treat each other kindly.

Ⓑ They try to get out of each other's way.

Ⓒ They complain about each other.

Ⓓ They blame Father for their troubles.

12. Father describes his life as _____ .

Ⓐ miserable   Ⓑ busy

Ⓒ difficult   Ⓓ hopeless

© Harcourt

Practice Book
On Your Mark

13. Why does the family bring a goat to live in the house?

Ⓐ It's easier for Mary Ann to milk the goat inside.

Ⓑ Father insists upon it.

Ⓒ Bartholomew tells them to do it.

Ⓓ The goat is cold outside.

14. Bartholomew is known throughout the village as _____ .

Ⓐ an old man   Ⓑ a crazy man

Ⓒ an animal lover   Ⓓ a wise man

15. What is one reason the goat doesn't work out?

Ⓐ Meg likes the goat.

Ⓑ Martin and Willy ignore it.

Ⓒ The goat attacks after being teased.

Ⓓ The goat provides enough milk.

16. When the family complains about the goat, Bartholomew tells them to _____ .

Ⓐ take the goat back outside

Ⓑ learn to get along with it

Ⓒ stop teasing it

Ⓓ bring the chickens inside, too

17. What does the family do when the chickens come inside?

Ⓐ They complain more than ever.

Ⓑ They begin to stop complaining.

Ⓒ They stay busy collecting eggs.

Ⓓ They blame the boys for their troubles.

18. Bartholomew tells the family to bring their donkey inside because he _____ .

Ⓐ doesn't want the donkey to be alone outside

Ⓑ wants the family to appreciate their farm animals

Ⓒ thinks the house has a little more room left

Ⓓ wants the family to know how much room they really have

19. Why does the family follow Bartholomew's advice even after it made things worse?

_____

_____

_____

_____

_____

20. What is the lesson or moral of the story?

_____

_____

_____

_____

_____

_____

Practice Book
On Your Mark

Leah's Pony

> **Directions:** For items 1–18, fill in the circle in front of the correct answer. For items 19–20, write the answer.

Vocabulary

1. In the recent election, we elected new _____ officials.
- Ⓐ bid
- Ⓑ galloped
- Ⓒ glistened
- Ⓓ county

2. The snowflakes _____ in the sunlight.
- Ⓐ glistened
- Ⓑ clutched
- Ⓒ galloped
- Ⓓ auctioneer

3. The cowboy was in a hurry, so he jumped on the fastest horse and _____ off.
- Ⓐ auctioneer
- Ⓑ galloped
- Ⓒ clutched
- Ⓓ glistened

4. The _____ was asking too much for the antique chair.
- Ⓐ galloped
- Ⓑ auctioneer
- Ⓒ glistened
- Ⓓ clutched

5. Mom _____ her handbag tightly as we walked through the mall.
- Ⓐ glistened
- Ⓑ county
- Ⓒ clutched
- Ⓓ bid

6. Father _____ on several chairs at the auction.
- Ⓐ bid
- Ⓑ galloped
- Ⓒ auctioneer
- Ⓓ glistened

Comprehension

7. This selection is most like _____ .
- Ⓐ a personal narrative
- Ⓑ an informational story
- Ⓒ a historical fiction
- Ⓓ a biography

8. Leah gets her pony "the year the corn grew tall and straight" because _____ .
- Ⓐ Papa needs a horse to round up the cattle
- Ⓑ Papa earns good money from selling the corn
- Ⓒ Leah has to go to town on errands
- Ⓓ Leah keeps asking for one

9. The year that the corn grew not taller than a man's thumb, things change in Leah's house because _____ .
- Ⓐ the family has no money
- Ⓑ the nights are hot and dry
- Ⓒ Papa is very sick
- Ⓓ Leah can't keep the pony's coat shining

10. The sky turns black some days because _____ .
- Ⓐ clouds cover the sky
- Ⓑ flocks of birds fly over
- Ⓒ dust fills the sky
- Ⓓ it rains hard

11. Why does Mama make underwear for Leah out of flour sacks?
- Ⓐ The sacks are a pretty color.
- Ⓑ The material is soft.
- Ⓒ There is no place to buy cloth.
- Ⓓ Mama has no money to buy cloth.

Grade 3-2

12. Papa borrows money from the bank to buy _____ .

   Ⓐ seeds   Ⓑ a tractor

   Ⓒ cattle   Ⓓ Leah's pony

13. Times are hard for farmers because _____ .

   Ⓐ the grasshoppers and the lack of rain have ruined their crops

   Ⓑ the farm equipment breaks and can't be fixed

   Ⓒ the farmers can't afford to buy seed

   Ⓓ all the farm animals get sick and die

14. What is the hardest thing for Papa to sell?

   Ⓐ Mama's rooster   Ⓑ the tractor

   Ⓒ his pickup truck   Ⓓ Leah's favorite calf

15. Leah thinks Mr. B. might buy her pony because he _____ .

   Ⓐ has a lot of money

   Ⓑ likes animals

   Ⓒ once asked her if he could buy the pony

   Ⓓ tells her the pony is the finest in the county

16. Who is the man in the big hat?

   Ⓐ a neighbor   Ⓑ Mr. B.

   Ⓒ the auctioneer   Ⓓ Papa

17. A penny auction occurs when people _____ .

   Ⓐ buy pennies for their coin collections

   Ⓑ buy valuable things for small amounts of money

   Ⓒ pay only a penny for each thing they buy

   Ⓓ pay a penny to watch the auction

Grade 3-2

Practice Book
On Your Mark

18. Which word best tells about Leah's neighbors?

Ⓐ curious   Ⓑ generous

Ⓒ careful   Ⓓ nosy

19. How does Leah plan to keep someone else from buying Papa's tractor?

_____

_____

_____

_____

_____

_____

20. After Leah bids on the tractor for her dad, what do the neighbors do next?

_____

_____

_____

_____

_____

_____

_____

Yippee-Yay!

Directions: For items 1–18, fill in the circle in front of the correct answer. For items 19–20, write the answer.

Vocabulary

1. Dad was outside _____ the roses to help them grow.
- Ⓐ corral
- Ⓑ tending
- Ⓒ profit
- Ⓓ market

2. The show horses are prancing around the _____ .
- Ⓐ stray
- Ⓑ profit
- Ⓒ tending
- Ⓓ corral

3. People who raise cattle for a living are called _____ .
- Ⓐ market
- Ⓑ corral
- Ⓒ profit
- Ⓓ ranchers

4. Our class made a _____ from the bake sale.
- Ⓐ market
- Ⓑ stray
- Ⓒ profit
- Ⓓ tending

5. Michael found a _____ dog on the way to school.
- Ⓐ stray
- Ⓑ market
- Ⓒ corral
- Ⓓ profit

6. My friends found some good fruit at a new _____ .
- Ⓐ ranchers
- Ⓑ stray
- Ⓒ tending
- Ⓓ market

Practice Book
On Your Mark

Grade 3-2

Comprehension

7. According to the selection, the main reason there were so few cowgirls in the Old West is because _____ .
Ⓐ cowgirls did not practice riding horses
Ⓑ the work was considered too harsh for girls
Ⓒ girls were too busy raising crops
Ⓓ the cattle were not used to being controlled by girls

8. From the 1860s to 1890s is considered in the Old West to be the era of _____ .
Ⓐ poor and undeveloped ranches
Ⓑ the American cowboy
Ⓒ the American cowgirl
Ⓓ short cattle drives to nearby railroads

9. In order to work, a cowhand had to own _____ .
Ⓐ a saddle　　　　　Ⓑ a horse
Ⓒ spurs　　　　　　Ⓓ a corral

10. What was a cowhand's most important skill?
Ⓐ busting horses　　Ⓑ riding horses
Ⓒ roping cattle　　　Ⓓ branding cattle

11. After cowhands rounded up the cattle, the next thing they did was _____ .
Ⓐ lasso the calves　　Ⓑ brand the herd
Ⓒ brand the calves　　Ⓓ count the herd

Practice Book
On Your Mark

12. Cowhands did not brand calves until after roundup because calves _____ .

Ⓐ were kept in a pen   Ⓑ followed their mothers

Ⓒ were too wild   Ⓓ would cause a stampede

13. Which group would <u>wrangler</u>, <u>cookie</u>, and <u>flank rider</u> belong to?

Ⓐ events at a rodeo

Ⓑ kinds of brands

Ⓒ jobs on a trail drive

Ⓓ clothing that cowhands wear

14. The drag position was the worst job because cowboys _____ .

Ⓐ had to ride longer than other cowhands

Ⓑ worked in the dust at the back of the herd

Ⓒ had to keep the herd moving

Ⓓ dragged the wagon full of food

15. What was the reason for a trail drive?

Ⓐ to move the herd to a different place for grazing

Ⓑ to keep the cattle from losing weight

Ⓒ to take the herd to a railroad station to be sold

Ⓓ to keep cattle from different ranches apart

16. There are no long cattle drives today because _____ .

Ⓐ houses have been built on the trails

Ⓑ the ranchers don't have to move their cattle

Ⓒ there aren't enough cowhands to do the work

Ⓓ railroads are close to the ranches

Grade 3-2

Practice Book
On Your Mark

17. What job do cowhands do today in a different way?

   Ⓐ branding calves   Ⓑ riding horseback

   Ⓒ roping steers   Ⓓ rounding up stray cattle

18. Why did the author write this book?

   Ⓐ to tell how exciting it is to be a cowhand

   Ⓑ to describe a cowhand's life in the late 1800s

   Ⓒ to explain that few girls were cowhands in the Wild West

   Ⓓ to convince people to become cowboys and cowgirls

19. Ranchers didn't have fences around all their land. Why not?

_____

_____

_____

_____

_____

20. Cattle from different ranches mixed together on the range. Explain how ranchers made sure they could identify their own cattle, including new calves.

_____

_____

_____

_____

Practice Book
On Your Mark

Boom Town

Directions: For items 1–18, fill in the circle in front of the correct answer. For items 19–20, write the answer.

Vocabulary

1. Many people traveled in a _____ during Old West times.
Ⓐ landmark   Ⓑ stagecoach
Ⓒ skillet   Ⓓ settle

2. On our trip to New York, we visited the Statue Of Liberty, a famous _____ .
Ⓐ boom town   Ⓑ skillet
Ⓒ landmark   Ⓓ stagecoach

3. In the Old West, a settlement often turned into a _____ .
Ⓐ boom town   Ⓑ settle
Ⓒ stagecoach   Ⓓ skillet

4. Every day, the _____ took their tools and went off to the gold mines.
Ⓐ nuggets   Ⓑ boom town
Ⓒ landmark   Ⓓ miners

5. The miners collected a pan full of gold _____ .
Ⓐ nuggets   Ⓑ skillet
Ⓒ settle   Ⓓ landmark

6. Uncle Jim makes pancakes in a _____ .
Ⓐ skillet   Ⓑ settle
Ⓒ landmark   Ⓓ nuggets

Grade 3-2

Practice Book
On Your Mark

Grade 3-2

7. The Browns want to _____ in a place where there are good schools.

Ⓐ landmark   Ⓑ stagecoach

Ⓒ settle   Ⓓ boom town

Comprehension

8. This selection takes place long ago in _____ .

Ⓐ California   Ⓑ Oregon

Ⓒ gold fields   Ⓓ St. Joe

9. Pa has brought his family out west because he thinks he'll _____ .

Ⓐ work all day without pay

Ⓑ strike it rich

Ⓒ make his wife happy

Ⓓ learn to read

10. Who is telling the story?

Ⓐ Ma   Ⓑ Pa

Ⓒ Baby Betsy   Ⓓ Amanda

11. In the selection, the phrase "Once in a while a crow flew by" shows how _____ life was.

Ⓐ boring   Ⓑ funny

Ⓒ beautiful   Ⓓ happy

12. Because Pa lives in the gold fields during the week, he _____ .

Ⓐ helps Amanda's pie business get started

Ⓑ makes crusts for the pies

Ⓒ can't find pans for Amanda

Ⓓ picks apples for the pies

13. Ma said it was unlikely that Amanda could make pie because _____ .
- Ⓐ there were no pie pans and there was no oven
- Ⓑ Amanda was poor at baking pies
- Ⓒ the boys would make fun of her
- Ⓓ there wasn't enough flour for a pie crust

14. Amanda was _____ about baking pies.
- Ⓐ angry
- Ⓑ foolish
- Ⓒ grateful
- Ⓓ persistent

15. The main reason Amanda was successful at baking her first pie was that _____ .
- Ⓐ Ma ended up making it for her
- Ⓑ her brothers finally decided to help
- Ⓒ Pa came home to encourage her
- Ⓓ she learned to solve her problem a different way

16. Pa came home with money on Saturday night because he had _____ .
- Ⓐ struck gold
- Ⓑ traded his horse
- Ⓒ sold Amanda's pie
- Ⓓ landed another job

17. Many of the miners decide that _____ .
- Ⓐ mining for gold is an easy way to get rich
- Ⓑ living apart from your family is too hard
- Ⓒ it is easier to get rich doing something else
- Ⓓ only young miners strike it rich

Practice Book
On Your Mark

18. The main purpose of this story is to show how a _____ .

(A) town gets its start

(B) little girl learns to bake

(C) family strikes it rich

(D) brother and sister can get along

19. Why would Amanda and other businesses need a bank in town?

_____

_____

_____

_____

_____

_____

20. Explain what Amanda did, other than bake pies, to turn the little settlement into a boom town.

_____

_____

_____

_____

_____

_____

Cocoa Ice

Directions: For items 1–18, fill in the circle in front of the correct answer. For items 19–20, write the answer.

Vocabulary

1. At the marine museum, we toured an old-fashioned _____ that was tied to the dock.
Ⓐ machete   Ⓑ trading
Ⓒ schooner   Ⓓ bargain

2. The _____ ship brought silk from China to sell in France.
Ⓐ pulp   Ⓑ harvest
Ⓒ machete   Ⓓ trading

3. In the autumn we _____ the apples.
Ⓐ harvest   Ⓑ schooner
Ⓒ trading   Ⓓ support

4. Christina had to use a _____ to cut the tall grass.
Ⓐ support   Ⓑ machete
Ⓒ bargain   Ⓓ schooner

5. My aunt says the best part of the orange is its _____ .
Ⓐ harvest   Ⓑ bargain
Ⓒ trading   Ⓓ pulp

6. Whenever there is a sale, Mom tries to find a good _____ .
Ⓐ bargain   Ⓑ harvest
Ⓒ support   Ⓓ pulp

7. The farmer staked the plants, as the tomatoes were heavy and the vines could not _____ them.

  Ⓐ bargain   Ⓑ trading

  Ⓒ support   Ⓓ machete

Comprehension

8. What two locations are talked about in the story?

  Ⓐ Santa Maria and Maine

  Ⓑ Santo Domingo and Maryland

  Ⓒ California and Maine

  Ⓓ Santo Domingo and Maine

9. What happens to the cocoa beans before they dry in the sun?

  Ⓐ They are split open with a machete.

  Ⓑ They are put between banana leaves with pulp.

  Ⓒ They are covered with turtle grass.

  Ⓓ They are put in a bowl of coconut milk.

10. Why is it necessary to dry the cocoa beans in the sun?

  Ⓐ Fresh beans smell bad.

  Ⓑ The pulp is poisonous.

  Ⓒ Fresh beans give you a toothache.

  Ⓓ Drying cocoa beans takes out the bitterness.

11. In this story, Mama steams conchs and picks out the meat. Conchs are a kind of _____ .

  Ⓐ bird   Ⓑ shellfish

  Ⓒ pan   Ⓓ rock

12. The island people trade for what they need by using all the following **except** _____ .

(A) ice

(B) cocoa beans

(C) coconuts

(D) bananas

13. Why is it important to be the first person to see a schooner come into the bay?

(A) The first people to reach a ship have a better chance of trading for what they want.

(B) Captains trade only with the first few people to arrive.

(C) When the ship gets crowded with people, there is a lot of pushing and shoving.

(D) Captains get angry if many people want to trade.

14. What must Jacob have traded to get the seashell on the mantel shelf?

(A) hay

(B) pictures of Maine

(C) ice

(D) the balsam bag

15. Papa and Uncle Jacob worry when it snows on the river because _____ .

(A) then they can't walk on the river

(B) then it is too cold to cut ice

(C) snow keeps the river from freezing

(D) horses can't walk on snow

16. The first step in harvesting the ice is _____ .

(A) lifting blocks of ice

(B) cutting through the ice to the water

(C) floating ice on the water

(D) making grooves in the ice

Practice Book
On Your Mark

17. Sailors cover the ice on schooners with sawdust and hay
to _____ .

   Ⓐ keep the ice from moving

   Ⓑ keep the ice clean

   Ⓒ keep the ice from melting

   Ⓓ make it easier to load the ice

18. How are the girl in Santo Domingo and the girl in Maine
alike?

   Ⓐ Both like chocolate.   Ⓑ Both climb trees.

   Ⓒ Both drink coconut milk.   Ⓓ Both swim in a river.

19. What are three amazing things about Maine, according to the
girl from Santo Domingo?

_____

_____

_____

_____

20. What are three amazing things about Santo Domingo,
according to the girl from Maine?

_____

_____

_____

_____

_____

Practice Book
On Your Mark

If You Made a Million

Directions: For items 1–18, fill in the circle in front of the correct answer. For items 19–20, write the answer.

Vocabulary

1. My parents offered _____ to all the graduates.
Ⓐ combinations   Ⓑ congratulations
Ⓒ amount   Ⓓ receive

2. My brother and I _____ our family's love above all else.
Ⓐ value   Ⓑ amount
Ⓒ choices   Ⓓ congratulations

3. What is the _____ I owe for the groceries?
Ⓐ receive   Ⓑ choices
Ⓒ combinations   Ⓓ amount

4. David will _____ an allowance every month.
Ⓐ amount   Ⓑ combinations
Ⓒ receive   Ⓓ choices

5. There are several _____ of coins that will equal twenty-five cents.
Ⓐ combinations   Ⓑ value
Ⓒ congratulations   Ⓓ receive

6. At the banquet, the _____ for dessert were ice cream or pudding.
Ⓐ amount   Ⓑ value
Ⓒ choices   Ⓓ receive

Grade 3-2

Comprehension

7. This selection is most like an _____ .

Ⓐ autograph 　　　　Ⓑ interview

Ⓒ informational book　Ⓓ advertisement

8. In this selection, what happens when you do one of the suggested jobs?

Ⓐ You win prizes.　　Ⓑ You get to make wishes.

Ⓒ You score points.　Ⓓ You earn money.

9. Which of the following combinations has the same value as one dollar?

Ⓐ ten dimes　　　　Ⓑ two quarters

Ⓒ five nickels　　　Ⓓ twenty pennies

10. You can earn the most interest from a bank by _____ .

Ⓐ leaving your money in the bank for a year

Ⓑ leaving your money in the bank for many years

Ⓒ doing jobs for the bank

Ⓓ getting paid with dollar bills

11. The author suggested using a check at times instead of money. In this selection, a <u>check</u> is a _____ .

Ⓐ pattern of squares on clothing

Ⓑ written order to a bank to pay money to someone

Ⓒ bill at a restaurant

Ⓓ mark that shows something is chosen

12. You give someone a check and that person puts it in his bank. Your check then goes to _____ .

Ⓐ a gas station   Ⓑ your bank

Ⓒ a clearinghouse   Ⓓ a store

13. When you borrow money from a bank, you must pay back _____ .

Ⓐ none of the money you borrowed

Ⓑ more money than you borrowed

Ⓒ as much money as you borrowed

Ⓓ less money than you borrowed

14. Your friend wants to sell you a bike for $50. Which sentence is an example of a down payment, according to this article?

Ⓐ You give your friend $10 and promise to pay her $10 a week for four more weeks.

Ⓑ You give your friend $60, and she gives you $10 back.

Ⓒ You give your friend $50.

Ⓓ You give your friend $25, and your dad gives her $25.

15. According to the selection, what is the largest bill made today?

Ⓐ $10   Ⓑ $50

Ⓒ $20   Ⓓ $100

16. The most important fact about having a million dollars is that _____ .

Ⓐ a million dollars in quarters weighs as much as a whale

Ⓑ it's not a lot of money

Ⓒ you can buy something very expensive with it

Ⓓ you need to decide whether to spend it or save it

Practice Book
On Your Mark

17. A million dollars in one-dollar bills would weigh _____ .
    Ⓐ over two tons   Ⓑ under 360 pounds
    Ⓒ over one ton   Ⓓ under one ton

18. Why did the author write this book?
    Ⓐ to tell a funny story
    Ⓑ to encourage readers to spend money
    Ⓒ to explain how the money system works
    Ⓓ to explain how to make a million dollars

19. Name three ways you can pay for things.

_____

_____

_____

_____

_____

20. There are two kinds of interest. Explain the difference between the interest for leaving money in the bank and the interest for borrowing money.

_____

_____

_____

_____

_____

_____

Practice Book
On Your Mark

I'm in Charge of Celebrations

Directions: For items 1–18, fill in the circle in front of the correct answer. For items 19–20, write the answer.

Vocabulary

1. I will _____ you when I am ready.
Ⓐ tracks   Ⓑ choosy
Ⓒ admiring   Ⓓ signal

2. Our town has big _____ on the Fourth of July and Labor Day.
Ⓐ tracks   Ⓑ admiring
Ⓒ celebrations   Ⓓ average

3. My parents are very _____ about the TV programs I am allowed to watch.
Ⓐ choosy   Ⓑ signal
Ⓒ celebrations   Ⓓ tracks

4. The doctor says the baby is _____ in height for her age.
Ⓐ admiring   Ⓑ choosy
Ⓒ average   Ⓓ celebrations

5. We knew there had been a raccoon in the yard last night because we saw its _____ .
Ⓐ choosy   Ⓑ tracks
Ⓒ admiring   Ⓓ average

6. The teacher was _____ Peter's artwork when we walked in.
Ⓐ signal   Ⓑ admiring
Ⓒ average   Ⓓ tracks

Grade 3-2

Comprehension

7. This selection is most like a narrative poem because it _____ .
  (A) is shaped like a camel
  (B) is a song
  (C) is a form of Japanese poetry
  (D) tells a story

8. The poet keeps track of the many events she celebrates
by _____ .
  (A) drawing pictures of them
  (B) keeping a notebook of important events
  (C) inviting animal friends to celebrations
  (D) painting in her diary every day

9. When the poet says "your heart will POUND," she means that
you will feel _____ .
  (A) scared   (B) sad
  (C) excited   (D) disappointed

10. <u>Swirling</u>, <u>swaying</u>, and <u>dancing</u> are ways that dust
devils _____ .
  (A) sound   (B) feel
  (C) move   (D) smell

11. A <u>dust devil</u> is a kind of _____ .
  (A) wind   (B) dirt
  (C) dance   (D) music

Grade 3-2

12. How do the <u>dust devils</u> affect the poet and her friends?

Ⓐ They turn around and around until they fall down.

Ⓑ They protect their faces from the dust.

Ⓒ They jump up and down like dust devils.

Ⓓ They drive the truck very fast to get away from the dust devils.

13. The poet draws the jackrabbit in her picture of the triple rainbow because _____ .

Ⓐ it is common to see a rabbit looking at rainbows

Ⓑ the rabbit looks silly in front of the rainbows

Ⓒ it is rare to see a rabbit standing on a hill

Ⓓ she has shared the experience with the jackrabbit

14. The poet feels lucky on Green Cloud Day because _____ .

Ⓐ the cloud has a parrot's shape

Ⓑ it doesn't rain on that day

Ⓒ she has the good fortune to see the cloud

Ⓓ it is a winter afternoon

15. The poet "never will feel quite the same" after seeing the coyote because _____ .

Ⓐ the coyote's howl is frightening

Ⓑ they look into each other's eyes

Ⓒ they walk side by side for a while

Ⓓ the writer touches the coyote

16. Where do the events that the poet celebrates take place?

Ⓐ by a pool of water   Ⓑ near a city

Ⓒ in the mountains   Ⓓ in a desert

Practice Book
On Your Mark

17. What sort of things does the poet celebrate?

Ⓐ things that she can count

Ⓑ things in nature

Ⓒ birthdays of famous people

Ⓓ important dates in history

18. Why does the poet laugh when people ask if she is lonely?

Ⓐ because she feels the land and animals are her friends

Ⓑ because most of the time she has many visitors

Ⓒ because she has many pets to keep her company

Ⓓ because she is a happy person

19. Describe the fireball that the poet sees during "The Time of the Falling Stars."

_____

_____

_____

_____

_____

20. How is the time when the poet celebrates New Year's different from the time many people celebrate?

_____

_____

_____

_____

_____

Practice Book
On Your Mark

Alejandro's Gift

Directions: For items 1–18, fill in the circle in front of the correct answer. For items 19–20, write the answer.

Vocabulary

1. The wind caused the blades of the _____ to go round and round.
Ⓐ furrows   Ⓑ ample
Ⓒ windmill   Ⓓ cherished

2. The little boy _____ each moment spent with his grandfather.
Ⓐ cherished   Ⓑ growth
Ⓒ ample   Ⓓ furrows

3. Dad dug _____ to plant the tomato seeds.
Ⓐ cherished   Ⓑ furrows
Ⓒ shunned   Ⓓ windmill

4. There was _____ room in the garden to plant carrots, too.
Ⓐ ample   Ⓑ shunned
Ⓒ windmill   Ⓓ admiring

5. Because my mother doesn't like crowds, she _____ the mall when it was busy.
Ⓐ cherished   Ⓑ ample
Ⓒ shunned   Ⓓ growth

6. In science class, we recorded each plant's weekly _____ in our notebooks.
Ⓐ furrows   Ⓑ cherished
Ⓒ ample   Ⓓ growth

Practice Book
On Your Mark

Grade 3-2

Comprehension

7. This selection is a good example of realistic fiction because _____ .

   Ⓐ the setting could be a real place

   Ⓑ many events are unrealistic

   Ⓒ the story was told orally before it was written

   Ⓓ the story involves technology from the future

8. Alejandro can have a garden in the desert because _____ .

   Ⓐ he does not have many visitors

   Ⓑ there is a water hole next to his house

   Ⓒ the windmill brings water up from his well

   Ⓓ he does not need much water for himself and his burro

9. Alejandro works in his garden for hours because _____ .

   Ⓐ the work keeps him from being lonely

   Ⓑ the garden is very big

   Ⓒ he wants the vegetables to grow quickly

   Ⓓ there are a lot of weeds in the garden

10. In this selection, woodpeckers, thrashers, and roadrunners are _____ .

   Ⓐ desert flowers   Ⓑ desert birds

   Ⓒ kinds of cactus   Ⓓ desert fruit

11. All the animals that come to the garden _____ .

   Ⓐ are small   Ⓑ have long tails

   Ⓒ have fur   Ⓓ have four legs

12. The squirrel comes to Alejandro's garden because it is _____ .

Ⓐ curious   Ⓑ lost

Ⓒ thirsty   Ⓓ hungry

13. Alejandro digs a water hole to _____ .

Ⓐ feed his animal visitors

Ⓑ provide water for the other, larger desert animals

Ⓒ water his garden more easily

Ⓓ get better water for his burro

14. When "the skunk darted to safety in the underbrush," _____ .

Ⓐ the skunk got caught

Ⓑ Alejandro did not understand why the skunk ran away

Ⓒ Alejandro realized that the animals did not feel safe near the house

Ⓓ the skunk warned other animals of danger

15. Animals ignore the first water hole because it is _____ .

Ⓐ salty   Ⓑ muddy

Ⓒ too shallow   Ⓓ in the open

16. Which word best tells about Alejandro?

Ⓐ defeated   Ⓑ determined

Ⓒ selfish   Ⓓ fearful

17. The second water hole is different from the first one Alejandro dug because it is _____ .

Ⓐ next to his house

Ⓑ sheltered from his house

Ⓒ smaller than the first one

Ⓓ shunned by the large animals

Grade 3-2

18. Alejandro knows when animals are at the second water hole because _____ .

Ⓐ they always come at the same time

Ⓑ his burro moves about

Ⓒ he can see them

Ⓓ he can hear them

19. How does Alejandro fix the problems with the first water hole?

_____

_____

_____

_____

_____

20. Explain the two meanings of the story's title, *Alejandro's Gift*. What gift does Alejandro intend to give? What gift does he receive?

_____

_____

_____

_____

_____

_____

Practice Book
On Your Mark

Rocking and Rolling

Directions: For items 1–18, fill in the circle in front of the correct answer. For items 19–20, write the answer.

Vocabulary

1. The molten material beneath the earth's crust is _____ .
Ⓐ range   Ⓑ epicenter
Ⓒ magma   Ⓓ peak

2. When I help with frosting the cookies, I make sure icing is placed right up to the _____ of each cookie.
Ⓐ edges   Ⓑ range
Ⓒ coast   Ⓓ magma

3. Do you know which mountain _____ is the highest in the world?
Ⓐ epicenter   Ⓑ range
Ⓒ magma   Ⓓ coast

4. During a recent earthquake, our town was only ten miles north of the earthquake's _____ .
Ⓐ range   Ⓑ magma
Ⓒ epicenter   Ⓓ coast

5. There are many beautiful beaches along the Florida _____ .
Ⓐ magma   Ⓑ peak
Ⓒ epicenter   Ⓓ coast

6. Mount McKinley is the highest mountain _____ in North America.
Ⓐ peak   Ⓑ edges
Ⓒ coast   Ⓓ magma

Practice Book
On Your Mark

Comprehension

7. Cracks in the block mountains are called _____ .

Ⓐ plates   Ⓑ bumps

Ⓒ humps   Ⓓ faults

8. How hot is the center of the earth?

Ⓐ 9°F   Ⓑ 90°F

Ⓒ 900°F   Ⓓ 9,000°F

9. The outermost layer of the earth is the crust. What is the next layer called?

Ⓐ mantle   Ⓑ outer core

Ⓒ inner core   Ⓓ plate

10. What is magma like?

Ⓐ the back of an elephant   Ⓑ a jigsaw puzzle

Ⓒ gooey oatmeal   Ⓓ an exploding bomb

11. Which sentence tells something true about the earth?

Ⓐ People have dug to the center of the earth.

Ⓑ The earth's plates have drifted apart.

Ⓒ There are no mountains under the ocean.

Ⓓ The earth's crust is made of metal.

12. An earthquake is caused by _____ .

Ⓐ a plate underground breaking away from another plate

Ⓑ outer layers of the earth pressing down on the inner core

Ⓒ a huge wave traveling miles through the ocean

Ⓓ magma forcing the earth's crust into a dome

Grade 3-2

© Harcourt

13. The shocks from an earthquake _____ .

Ⓐ shoot up like flames from a fire

Ⓑ go around in circles like a ball at the end of a string

Ⓒ work outward like ripples from a stone thrown in a lake

Ⓓ build up a wall of mud sliding into a building

14. How many earthquakes cause damage?

Ⓐ most of them   Ⓑ a few of them

Ⓒ none of them   Ⓓ all of them

15. All of the following are types of mountains **except** _____ .

Ⓐ fold   Ⓑ dome

Ⓒ ridge   Ⓓ block

16. Mount Everest will grow taller because _____ .

Ⓐ it sits on cracks in a plate

Ⓑ wind will shape huge ridges

Ⓒ India continues to push northward

Ⓓ magma will bulge up under the crust and cause a hump

17. The author compares the power of wind erosion to that of _____ .

Ⓐ an explosion   Ⓑ sandpaper

Ⓒ a flood   Ⓓ a blizzard

18. Why did the author write this article?

Ⓐ to warn people about dangerous places to live

Ⓑ to scare people

Ⓒ to explain the weather

Ⓓ to explain what is happening to the earth

Practice Book
On Your Mark

19. Why is there a National Disaster Prevention Day every year in Japan?

_____

_____

_____

_____

_____

_____

_____

_____

20. What occurs when an earthquake happens under land? under water?

_____

_____

_____

_____

_____

_____

_____

_____

The Armadillo from Amarillo

Directions: For items 1–18, fill in the circle in front of the correct answer. For items 19–20, write the answer.

Vocabulary

1. It seemed like it took forever, but we _____ arrived at the airport.
   (A) homeward
   (B) universe
   (C) eventually
   (D) converse

2. When the teenagers _____ too much in class, they get into trouble.
   (A) converse
   (B) sphere
   (C) homeward
   (D) eventually

3. On which _____ do you find the United States?
   (A) eventually
   (B) homeward
   (C) converse
   (D) continent

4. The new globe in our classroom is a giant _____ .
   (A) universe
   (B) converse
   (C) sphere
   (D) continent

5. The Earth is just a tiny part of the _____ .
   (A) converse
   (B) sphere
   (C) universe
   (D) eventually

6. The astronauts, after visiting the moon, turned the spaceship _____ .
   (A) homeward
   (B) universe
   (C) sphere
   (D) continent

Practice Book
On Your Mark

Comprehension

7. All of the following are reasons that this selection is fantasy **except** _____ .

Ⓐ it presents factual information

Ⓑ the characters are unreal

Ⓒ the events can't really happen

Ⓓ its purpose is to entertain

8. Sasparillo leaves home because he wants to _____ .

Ⓐ visit Brillo   Ⓑ explore the world

Ⓒ see a city   Ⓓ climb a tower

9. Who is Brillo?

Ⓐ a zookeeper   Ⓑ an eagle

Ⓒ an armadillo   Ⓓ a wild turkey

10. Sasparillo feels that the land near Amarillo is too _____ .

Ⓐ high and cool   Ⓑ wet and hot

Ⓒ hilly and hot   Ⓓ flat and cool

11. In this selection, Austin, Abilene, and Lubbock are places in _____ .

Ⓐ California   Ⓑ Louisiana

Ⓒ Texas   Ⓓ Arkansas

12. Sasparillo wants to ride on the eagle's back to _____ .

Ⓐ get a bigger view of the land

Ⓑ see how it feels to fly

Ⓒ take a rest from walking

Ⓓ feel the cool air up high

13. After they see the city of Amarillo, Sasparillo and Eagle next see the _____ .

   Ⓐ state of Texas

   Ⓑ United States of America

   Ⓒ North American continent

   Ⓓ planet Earth

14. Which of the following could not happen in real life?

   Ⓐ a rocket shuttle heading into space

   Ⓑ an eagle flying fast enough to catch a rocket ship

   Ⓒ craters existing on the moon

   Ⓓ Texas being one of the fifty states

15. How does Armadillo finally get to see where in the world he is?

   Ⓐ He gets Eagle to give him a ride.

   Ⓑ He climbs up canyon walls.

   Ⓒ He goes to the top of the tallest building in San Antonio.

   Ⓓ He rides on a spaceship into outer space.

16. How does Armadillo change after he sees where he is on Earth?

   Ⓐ He and Eagle stop being friends.

   Ⓑ He wants to travel to more new places.

   Ⓒ He is ready to go home.

   Ⓓ He wants to travel alone again.

17. Which word best tells about Armadillo?

   Ⓐ curious   Ⓑ lazy

   Ⓒ scared   Ⓓ jealous

18. What is the most important thing Sasparillo learns from his traveling?

    Ⓐ how many planets there are

    Ⓑ how thin the air in space is

    Ⓒ where his place in the world is

    Ⓓ how rockets are launched

19. What does the name Amarillo mean, and why do you think the city is called this?

_____

_____

_____

_____

_____

_____

20. Describe what Earth looks like from space.

_____

_____

_____

_____

_____

_____

_____

Visitors from Space

> **Directions:** For items 1–18, fill in the circle in front of the correct answer. For items 19–20, write the answer.

Vocabulary

1. He hit the ball with such _____ that you could hear the crack of the bat.
   - Ⓐ nucleus
   - Ⓑ force
   - Ⓒ loops
   - Ⓓ particles

2. The center, or _____, of the star looked extremely bright.
   - Ⓐ nucleus
   - Ⓑ solar wind
   - Ⓒ particles
   - Ⓓ force

3. Cowboy Charlie made huge _____ with his lasso.
   - Ⓐ fluorescent
   - Ⓑ particles
   - Ⓒ nucleus
   - Ⓓ loops

4. The _____ is a force from the Sun.
   - Ⓐ nucleus
   - Ⓑ fluorescent
   - Ⓒ solar wind
   - Ⓓ loops

5. The sawdust _____ flew around the garage when dad sawed the piece of wood.
   - Ⓐ particles
   - Ⓑ force
   - Ⓒ loops
   - Ⓓ nucleus

6. The new _____ lights brighten up the classroom.
   - Ⓐ force
   - Ⓑ solar wind
   - Ⓒ loops
   - Ⓓ fluorescent

Comprehension

7. The main purpose of this selection is to tell about _____ .
- Ⓐ traveling comets that can change our lives
- Ⓑ when the next solar system will appear in the universe
- Ⓒ what comets are made of and how they move and change
- Ⓓ how to become an astronomer and learn to write books

8. This selection is most like an informational book because it _____ .
- Ⓐ gives information about the solar system
- Ⓑ is written in the first person
- Ⓒ tells how to make something
- Ⓓ took place long ago

9. What does a comet look like in the sky?
- Ⓐ a group of stars
- Ⓑ the sun
- Ⓒ a flaming ball
- Ⓓ a full moon

10. Long ago, why did people think a comet was a warning of something bad?
- Ⓐ Comets appeared in the sky suddenly.
- Ⓑ People did not understand comets.
- Ⓒ Earthquakes and floods occurred after a comet appeared.
- Ⓓ Bad things always happened after a comet appeared.

11. The gas in the comet's coma can be compared to the gas in a _____ .
- Ⓐ shooting star
- Ⓑ dirty snowball
- Ⓒ solar wind
- Ⓓ fluorescent light bulb

Practice Book
On Your Mark

12. Scientists who study the planets and stars are called _____ .
   Ⓐ doctors   Ⓑ astronauts
   Ⓒ astronomers   Ⓓ dentists

13. Where do scientists think a huge cloud of comets might be?
   Ⓐ past the farthest planet   Ⓑ behind the moon
   Ⓒ around the sun   Ⓓ between the planets

14. The force that connects the solar system to the sun is called _____ .
   Ⓐ a coma   Ⓑ an asteroid
   Ⓒ gravity   Ⓓ a planet

15. What is the name for the "flying rocks" in our solar system?
   Ⓐ comets   Ⓑ meteors
   Ⓒ boulders   Ⓓ asteroids

16. A comet starts out as _____ .
   Ⓐ a large rock   Ⓑ a ball of frozen gases
   Ⓒ chunks of ice   Ⓓ a star

17. The tails of comets are made of _____ .
   Ⓐ gas and dust   Ⓑ rocks
   Ⓒ ice   Ⓓ dust

18. What is the name for the orbits that comets take around the sun?
   Ⓐ loops   Ⓑ periods
   Ⓒ ellipses   Ⓓ years

Grade 3-2

Practice Book
On Your Mark

Grade 3-2

19. What is one thing that makes a comet glow?

_____

_____

_____

_____

_____

_____

_____

_____

20. What is a comet tail?

_____

_____

_____

_____

_____

_____

_____

_____

Practice Book
On Your Mark